C000181106

100 WA...
Essex

compiled by

ANITA TOTHAM

The Crowood Press

First published in 1995 by
The Crowood Press Ltd
Ramsbury
Marlborough
Wiltshire SN8 2HR

This impression 2000

British Library Cataloguing-in-Publication Data
A catalogue record for this book is
available from the British Library

ISBN 1 85223 873 9

All maps by Janet Powell

Typeset by Carreg Limited, Ross-on-Wye, Herefordshire

Printed by Redwood Books, Trowbridge, Wiltshire

Contents

35.	The Dunmows	4$^1/_2$m	(7km)
36.	... and longer version	6$^1/_2$m	(10km)
37.	Little Baddow	4$^1/_2$m	(7km)
38.	Alresford	4$^1/_2$m	(7km)
39.	Blackmore	4$^1/_2$m	(7km)
40.	Nazeing	4$^1/_2$m	(7km)
41.	Tiptree	4$^1/_2$m	(7km)
42.	Mayland Creek	4$^1/_2$m	(7km)
43.	... and longer version	9m	(14$^1/_2$km)
44.	Ridgewell and Birdbrook	4$^1/_2$m	(7km)
45.	Matching Tye Green	4$^1/_2$m	(7km)
46.	Thaxted	4$^1/_2$m	(7km)
47.	Great Hallingbury	4$^1/_2$m	(7km)
48.	Lawford	5m	(8km)
49.	Dedham	5m	(8km)
50.	Stourdale	5m	(8km)
51.	Horkesley Heath	5m	(8km)
52.	West Bergholt	5m	(8km)
53.	Fordham	5m	(8km)
54.	Fairstead	5m	(8km)
55.	Terling	5m	(8km)
56.	Great Waltham	5m	(8km)
57.	Margaret Roding	5m	(8km)
58.	High Ongar	5m	(8km)
59.	Bradwell-on-Sea	5m	(8km)
60.	Heybridge Basin	5m	(8km)
61.	Castle Hedingham	5m	(8km)
62.	... and longer version	7m	(11km)
63.	Stock	5m	(8km)
64.	Tollesbury	5m	(8km)
65.	Tillingham	5m	(8km)
66.	Toppesfield	5m	(8km)
67.	Beaumont Quay	5m	(8km)
68.	Hadstock	5m	(8km)
69.	Abberton	5m	(8km)
70.	Finchingfield	5m	(8km)

Publisher's Note

We very much hope that you enjoy the routes presented in this book, which has been compiled with the aim of allowing you to explore the area in the best possible way - on foot.

We strongly recommend that you take the relevant map for the area, and for this reason we list the appropriate Ordnance Survey maps for each route. Whilst the details and descriptions given for each walk were accurate at time of writing, the countryside is constantly changing, and a map will be essential if, for any reason, you are unable to follow the given route. It is good practice to carry a map and use it so that you are always aware of your exact location.

We cannot be held responsible if some of the details in the route descriptions are found to be inaccurate, but should be grateful if walkers would advise us of any major alterations. Please note that whenever you are walking in the countryside you are on somebody else's land, and we must stress that you should *always* keep to established rights of way, and *never* cross fences, hedges or other boundaries unless there is a clear crossing point.

Remember the country code:

Enjoy the country and respect its life and work
Guard against all risk of fire
Fasten all gates
Keep dogs under close control
Keep to public footpaths across all farmland
Use gates and stiles to cross field boundaries
Leave all livestock, machinery and crops alone
Take your litter home
Help to keep all water clean
Protect wildlife, plants and trees
Make no unnecessary noise

The walks are listed by length - from approximately 3 to 9 miles - but the amount of time taken will depend on the fitness of the walkers and the time spent exploring any points of interest along the way. Nearly all the walks are circular and most offer recommendations for refreshments.

Good walking.

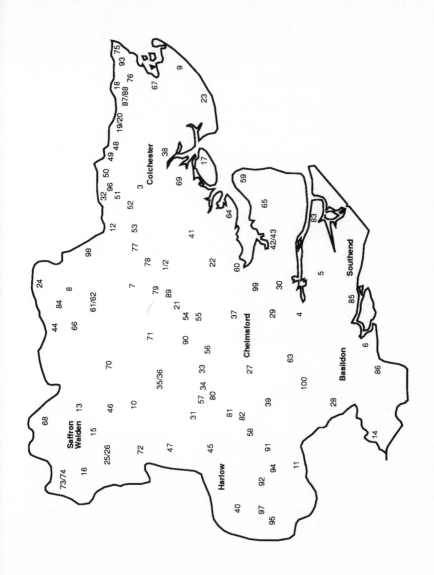

75
93
18
87/88 76
19/20
67
9
49 48
23
50
96
32 51 38
Colchester
12 52 3
98 53 17
77 69
78 59
7 1/2 41
79 64 65
89 22 42/43
84 8 21 60 83
24 54 99 30
44 66 61/62 55 37 5 Southend
70 90 56 29 4
71 27 Chelmsford 85
35/36 33 63 6
13 46 10 34 57 100 86
68 15 31 80 39
25/26 72 81 28
73/74 16 47 58 82 Basildon
45 91 14
Saffron 92 94 11
Walden Harlow
40 97
95

Maps: OS Sheets Landranger 168; Pathfinder 1076.
Historic Coggeshall, a crossing place for modern walking routes.
Start: At 850226, Stoneham Street car park, Coggeshall.

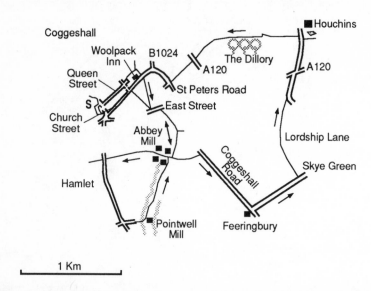

The car park is behind the clock, the entrance being up Stoneham Street, beside the library, housed in a former church.

Go out of the car park the way you came in, cross over in front of the library and walk the length of Queen Street. Cross the Vane Lane/Jaggards Road junction to enter the churchyard. Leave by the lych gate and cross the road to reach a path heading southwards beside the school's fence. Go through the recreation ground, turn left along East Street and, after 200 yards, turn right along a path that continues southward. Follow the path to a cross-paths by Abbey Mill. Turn right over leat and river bridges and walk through the working farmyard with caution. Climb Abbey Lane, passing **St Nicholas' Chapel**, to the right, to reach Coggeshall Hamlet. Turn left along the B1024 to a cross-roads. Turn left down Pointwell Lane, continuing along the drive to Pointwell

8

Mill. Go around the corner of the mill house, as waymarked, and walk with the upper water level on your left-hand side. Go over bridges and stiles to return to the cross-paths reached on the outward route.

The shorter route now retraces the outward route to the point where East Street was reached. Now, instead of retracing the outward path through the recreation ground, take the tarmac path that heads north-west to Horn Lane and Church Street. Turn left, downhill, to the clocktower. A pedestrians' entrance to the car park is through the Chapel Hotel's yard beside the clock.

The longer route turns right up a headland path to reach Coggeshall Road. Turn right, with care, as far as Feeringbury, on the right. There, turn left up a lane towards Skye Green. At the lane's crest take a bridleway (Lordship Lane) beside the first dwelling on the left. Follow this to Old Road. Cross the A120, with great care, to reach Houchins Lane. Follow the lane to reach a crossing path, by a reservoir, just before double jetted Houchins is reached. Turn left along the path, swapping sides of a ditch over a new plank bridge before The Dillory's trees are reached. Continue along the path to reach a stepped crossing of the A120. Please take care. Continue along the hedgeside path, then cross a mid-field path to reach St Peter's Road, **Coggeshall**. Turn right, then left at Church Green roundabout. Walk past the Woolpack Inn, continuing downhill on Church Street to reach the clock tower and the car park.

POINTS OF INTEREST:
St Nicholas' Chapel – An abbey, a Savigny house, was founded here in 1140 by King Stephen. In 1148 it joined the Cistercians, an Order which re-introduced the use of brick to our architecture. By the time of its Dissolution in 1538, the Abbey held 50,000 acres of land, mainly used for sheep rearing. St Nicholas' Chapel is a reminder of the former glory.

Coggeshall – Lace making reached a peak in Coggeshall during the 1870s when about fifty women were employed making a particular style of lace using a rectangular tambour. Three long walking routes pass through this fine village: the 75 mile Hadleigh Way, the 87 mile Essex Way, and the 130 mile Mucking Ugley Way.

REFRESHMENTS:
Many tastes are catered for in Coggeshall.

Maps: OS Sheets Landranger 168; Pathfinder 1077.
A walk in Britain's oldest recorded town.
Start: At 994255, Middleborough roundabout, Colchester.

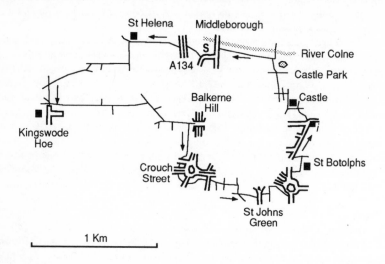

Enter Sheepen Place and underpass the A134. When you are by St Helena School, cross to the hedged path on the west side of the Institute of Further Education. After about 200 yards, look for the stile opposite a pedestrian gate in the Institute's fence: go over and turn right along a tarmac surface. Where this bends, continue ahead to swing left around an old pit. Rise southwards to reach a seat, a good vantage point, by a line of old fence posts. Trace the fence line around to the Kingswode Hoe stile by Sussex Road. Go left, with New Kiln Road hedge on your right, and dip to the stile. Climb up the triangular plot to Popes Lane. Go left, and approach the A134 footbridge over to The Hole in the Wall. Walk the west side of Balkerne Hill to observe the Roman gateway and wall, and St Mary's bi-coloured tower. Humpty, a cannon launcher, was knocked off with the tower-top during the 1648 Seige of Colchester. The tower was rebuilt long after the King's men had departed, leaving their nursery rhyme behind them. At the pedestrian crossing turn right to the Kings Arms. Cross Crouch Street and negotiate the roundabout anti-clockwise, using the underpass, and then cross Maldon Road to the Police Station's remains of a 4th-century Christian church. Pass southside of The Salvation Army HQ on Wellington Street and cross Chapel Street to Cedars Road. Turn up and around Walsingham Road to go left on Flagstaff Road to enter St John's Green, near the 1095 Benedictine Abbey gate.

Leave the Green eastwards from the Abbey Arms to reach St Botolph's Circus. Cross the B1025 and underpass via the circus gardens to reach Town Station. Turn left to veer northwards up St Botolph's Street, turning right on St Botolph's Church Walk. Go through the Augustinian Priory grounds to reach Priory Street, where the car park is bounded by the Roman Wall hardcore. Turn left, then right by South Gate, demolished in 1818, along Queen Street to the cluster of Museums, Art Gallery, Tourist Office and War Memorial by the **Castle**. Enter the Castle Park, leaving by the gate north-west of the Keep. Cross Ryegate Road to reach St Helen's Chapel dated 1097. Nearby is a Roman theatre site etched in Maidenburgh Street's paving stone contrasts. Down Maidenburgh Street is North Gate: round the Park's railings to Middlemill. Turn left and walk either bank of the River Colne to North Station Road bridge at Middleborough.

POINTS OF INTEREST:

Castle – The decapitated remains of the great Norman Keep are on the site of the Roman Claudius Temple. Both structures were the largest of their European contemporaries. The Temple was destroyed during Boadicea's rebellion. Much Roman material was used a millennium later by the Normans to build a Keep larger than London's White Tower. The missing upper tower material was removed during the next millennium for use in construction works elsewhere. The fascinating story of lost and refound knowledge of the site is told in the Castle Museum.

Camulodunum is the pre-Roman name for Britain's oldest recorded town. A pedestrian route of 21 miles around the town has been labelled with a P to give The Camuplodunum. There is also an Outer Camuplodunum of 42 miles and this Inner Camuplodunum of 3 miles.

REFRESHMENTS:
Most tastes are catered for in Colchester.

Maps: OS Sheets Landranger 167, Pathfinder 1142.
A walk to the first bridge over the tidal Crouch
Start: At 780947, the lay-by in Maltings Lane, Battlesbridge.

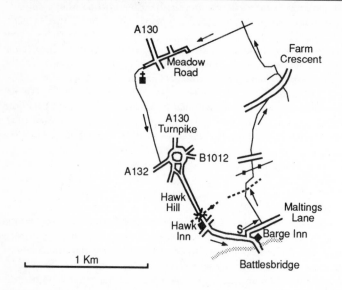

The nearby, larger car park is for patrons of the Antiques Centre in the attractive warehouses.

Go along Maltings Lane, away from **Battlesbridge**, until you are opposite Crouch Cottage. Turn left into a field and follow the left-hand hedge to the railway line. Veer right to the ramped footbridge, cross the Southminster branch line and turn right to walk beside the railway fence until you are opposite a pylon. Now walk mid-field by the pylon base to follow a series of white-capped posts marking the path to Farm Crescent. Go over a waymarked stile on to the new B1012, cross and go over the waymarked stile opposite. Cross to a stiled, waymarked footbridge in the north-west corner of the meadow. Cross and walk to the next waymarker by the transformer on stilts near the old B1012 filling station. Go through a gap and turn right along the road as far as Farm Crescent.

The path now continues northwards, going ahead off the left bend between garden fences, and rounding a back fence to reach a footbridge to Farm Spinney. Cross and climb under the trees, continuing, with a hedge on the left, to reach a cross-paths. Turn left. Magnificent oak trees line the vestigal hedgerow beside the track: follow the track to 63 Meadow Road. Use the sidewalk to reach the busy A130. Although the required Church Chase is directly across the road, it is better to move up the hill to use the controlled road crossing by the school, coming back down the hill before approaching All Saints' church.

Pass through the peaceful churchyard to reach a stile to the west of the tower. Go over and turn left by the farmstead fencing, moving over to get to the west of the hedgeline below the old military pillbox. Going back down towards the Crouch, there is a stile by another pillbox, separating the two fields. The A132 is reached by the huge roundabout (the Rettendon Turnpike) directional signboard. Dropped kerbs and tarmac paths show the anti-clockwise way across the A132 and the A130, although great care is still needed. Enter the orifice of Hawk Hill and walk downhill under the railway line. Turn left into **Maltings Lane** to return to the start.

POINTS OF INTEREST

Battlesbridge – Tidal power has been harnessed for various milling work at Battlesbridge for a long time. Though the tidal movement is free, the operation was inefficient because the power wheel was upstream of the bridge, a tantalising 100 yards away from the trans-shipping depot downstream of the same non-swinging bridge. The locking pool is visible today. Tidal power eventually gave way to oil and coal powered mills. The fine, tall Matthews Mill was demolished almost 20 years ago to break the continuity of provender preparation going back many years. Initially the provision was at Spitalfields outside the walls of London. Then, as London grew, it moved to Harold Wood, and when land transport expanded the city further, it re-sited to Battlesbridge.

Maltings Lane – Several of the warehouses around the sailing port of Battlesbridge have adapted well to the antiques trade, both wholesale and retail. Maltings Lane is a honeypot for browsing would-be buyers and some 80 dealers in the widest range of collectables. Nearby is The Barge, clad in traditional Essex black weather-boarding. It fits well in the scene of gathered memorabilia.

REFRESHMENTS
The Barge, Battlesbridge.
The Hawk, Battlesbridge.
There is also an Antiques Centre Teabar in Battlesbridge.

Maps: OS Sheets Landranger 178; Pathfinder 1143.
Over the sylvan Crouch-Roach watershed.
Start: At 840925, the Library Car Park, Hockley.

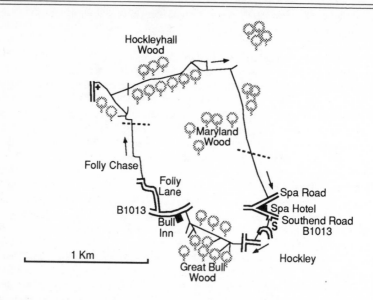

Leave the car park via the southern exit and fork right to pass the veterinary surgery up the tarmac path extension off Woodpond Avenue cul-de-sac. Turn right opposite 23 Kilnwood Avenue and turn left along Woodlands Road. Path 14 bissects dwellings 48 & 48A: take this to a footbridge at the rear of their garden fences. Go over into Great Bull Wood, part of the **Hockley Woods** complex. This is a free access woodland with several waymarked trails. Follow the perimeter path to the right, staying under the fringe of the canopy to walk around to the northern exit on to Main Road. Turn left, passing the Bull Inn. Where the B1013 becomes Alderman's Hill, Folly Lane branches off to the right. Take this road, following it around to the red letterbox. Here, Folly Chase veers off northwards: follow it, and where the tarmac finishes, at Hockley Vale Paddocks, follow an earthen path to the right, heading northwards again.

Follow the path beside paddock hedges to reach the white gates of a bridge over the electrified railway. Cross to the elbow of unmade St Peters Road.

Turn right, passing Hawthorns, and, when opposite Normandy, fork left along another earthen path enclosed by hedges. Note the right turn by the large oak tree and continue to Hockley church, a good viewing point. Return to the oak tree noted earlier, and turn left along the Mill Hill path to reach Hockleyhall Wood. The woodland is entered along a track used by vehicles from St Peters Road. The track swings right, uphill, before an earthen bank: walk over the bank, the boundary with Crabtree Wood, from where a more pleasant, pedestrian path is followed to the northern tip of the wood. Ditches as well as the path pass through the wood: bridges and log steps help the walker reach the exit to the eastern edge. From here a hedge-side path passes around the next field's corner to reach a new footbridge. Head eastwards mid-field for the pole by a convex hedge corner to reach a path junction.

Turn right, southwards, under the wires, heading for Maryland Wood. The first block of trees on the left gives way to garden rear fencing: continue to a footbridge with steps and cross into a coppice. The wires terminate at a transformer on stilts by the white gates of a level crossing of the railway. Cross, with great care, and climb the cutting steps by Hockley Business park. Now follow the left-hand fence out to a gap between 23 and 25 Spa Road. Turn right, uphill, to the **Spa Hotel**: the car park is reached across the Southend Road pedestrian crossing.

POINTS OF INTEREST:
Hockley Woods – The woods are owned and managed by Rochford District Council to make an optimum wildlife habitat balanced with providing maximum free access in a district of high population density. The woodlands are very ancient, the oldest in the county, and probably date from the last Ice Age. Coppice clearing takes place each year, using different areas of the wood on a 20 year cycle.

An excursion in to the woodland will reveal several continuous earthen banks threading though the trees. These are thought to be old manorial boundaries, which because of their protection by the trees, have not been ploughed out.

Spa Hotel – In 1842, a pump room was built to use waters from a spring said to have beneficial properties. The Spa Hotel was built soon after.

REFRESHMENTS:
The Spa Hotel, Hockley.
The Bull Inn, Hockley.

Walk 6   CORRINGHAM AND FOBBING   3m (5km)

Maps: OS Sheets Landranger 178; Pathfinder 1161.
The seat of the 1381 Peasants' Revolt.
Start: At 710831, Rookery Hill, Corringham.

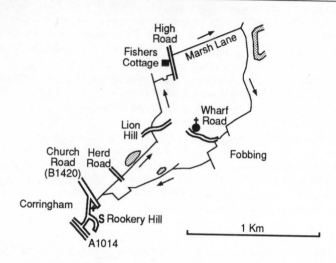

Walk to the B1420 and go uphill to St Mary's Church. Follow the path that crosses the churchyard to the Bull Inn. Head north-eastwards along the lane passing to the south of the inn. Pass between the schools on either side of Herd Road and go along the fenced path by a pitscape. Go over a stile to the cleft separating Corringham from Fobbing, staying by the mesh fence to reach a concrete road. Turn left to Lion Hill. Cross and follow Path 23, a re-instated mid-field path, to reach a transformer on stilts in the north-east corner of the field. Go through the gap west of Tripat Close, and follow the hedge one pole further northwards to the waymarker for Path 55. Turn right and wind around a pillbox to reach High Road by the Fobbing Lodge bus stops. Turn left and walk one bus stop to the timbered, jetted and thatched Fishers 1350 Cottage, to reach Marsh Lane, to the right, opposite No. 8 Mill Cottages. Follow the lane down to marshland, and where it bends left, go over the stile beside the gate ahead. Follow the level marshland path beyond to approach Fobbing Hall. In the first field, the path is nearer the flash of floodland water than the right-hand hedge. Go over a cartbridge into the next, huge field. Follow a path aligned with overhead wires until the poles begin to rise from base level, then change to a south-eastwards direction and to head for the hedge before the pylon cables.

When a hedge is reached, go right, and from the hedge end, go right again along a grassy headland towards St Michael's Church in **Fobbing**. When one field short of the church, turn left by a pond. Go a few paces beyond a willow tree, then turn right over a stile. Cross to the next stile between a stockyard wall and a garage, and go over on to Fobbing Hall's drive. Follow it to a white gate on to Wharf Road. Walk ahead to reach Latch End, the second dwelling on the left. Take the paved path that bends south behind the garden, following it to a stile. Go over and, a few paces southward along an earthen bank, turn right at a junction to go along Path 143. Cross a causeway to merge with another path. Maintain direction with a pond's chainlink fencing on the right. Merge with a track coming up from the marshes, and where that track bends right by a car park, get southside of a hedge to approach Corringham Hall. Watch for a school field to the right, and turn to walk alongside its western fence. When you are near the school buildings, go over stiles to cross a paddock to the left, heading towards a transformer on the lane to the south of the Bull Inn, **Corringham**. Cross the road and the churchyard and swing left to Rookery Hill.

POINTS OF INTEREST:

Fobbing – The events which began here on 30 May 1381 have been named, some say incorrectly, the Peasants' Revolt. Thomas Bampton, an important figure from Brentwood, entered Fobbing with his men to collect Poll Tax arrears. He was confident of his powers and liberal with his threats of punishment for non-payers, but he underestimated the stubborn sense of injustice felt in the tightly-knit fishing community, and aroused a vigorous response which saw his return to Brentwood empty-handed. A fuller story is told in the museum across the creek in Pitsea.

Corringham – Both Corringham and Fobbing cling to the rise of land from the Thames-side marshes, with views over a fine wilderness. Lining the Thames seaway across the marshes are the oil terminals, storage tanks and chemical factories of Canvey Island, Coryton and Thameshaven. The buildings have a certain beauty; but the fear of sudden explosion, or of imperceptible pollution, pervades the neighbourhood.

REFRESHMENTS
The White Lion Inn, Fobbing.
The Bull Inn, Corringham.

17

Walk 7   GREENSTEAD GREEN   3m (5km)

Maps: OS Sheets Landranger 168; Pathfinder 1076.
Greenstead Green in the Bourne Brook valley.
Start: At 822278, the Green in Greenstead Green.

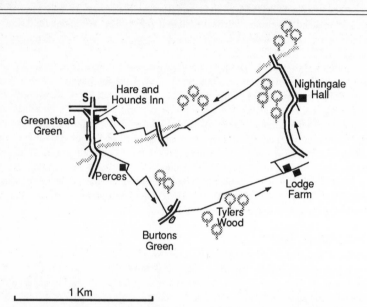

Descend Grange Hill, passing the Hare and Hounds Inn and the **Greenstead Green**
Village Hall and crossing Bourne Brook at the bottom. The road immediately swings
right up by Bournebrook **fuschia nursery**. Do not follow it: instead, go straight ahead
along a drive to Perces and Home Farm (this is Path 47). Follow the metal railings
around by the cedar tree to reach a black barn. Turn left in front of the bungalow, and
follow the metal railings down to a gate on a bridge. Cross into grazing, but after 20
yards turn right over a double stile and footbridge. Climb a small grazing plot, pass an
ash tree and go over a stile separated from the arable field by a fallen tree bole. This
is a nice quiet spot from which to watch the clouds chasing shadows across the
landscape.

    Follow the right-hand hedge to some ponds at Burtons Green. Go left, along the
road, for about 20 yards, then fork right, by a small green, along a path with a ditch to

the right separating it from the countryside premium set-aside meadow. Beyond the meadow is Tylers Wood. In the corner of the field, turn away from the wood to reach a footbridge. Cross and follow a mid-field path ENE by the solitary tree. Now head for the left-hand side of Lodge Farm's large buildings to reach a cartbridge over the incised stream. Cross and follow a change-crop alignment up to Lodge Farm. When you reach the newly planted hedge, turn left off the drive to cross a field, guided by diversion signs, to reach a gap by Nightingale Hall Farm Cottage. Turn left along a lane to re-enter the wooded valley of Bourne Brook.

Go around the bottom bend, by Bush Cottage, and as the lane swings right to bridge the brook, cross the footbridge straight ahead. Now follow Path 2 along the upper side of the brook-side hedge. Cross bridges over feeder streams as far as the path junction opposite New Wood. Here, a gap in the hedge allows both paths to enter the narrow, lower field. The parish boundary ditch must now be crossed, and neither parish has provided a bridge. The best available temporary route may be nearer the brook. Path 33 now crosses the rough grassy tussocks to reach a stile on to a road. Go right, over a bridge, to reach Path 34, to the left. Walk along the field edge to reach a spinney, and turn right up to the AWA treatment plant. Turn left to pass the compound – it is on your right-hand side. Now from the north-west corner of the spinney, cross a field towards a stile in the railings, backed by a white cottage a further field away. Do not cross the stile; instead, turn to climb along the left-hand hedge. Where the edge veers towards the dwelling with the double pitched gable, Path 46 turns left, between fences, to reach the Hare and Hounds Inn. Now reverse the outward route for the last few yards back to the start.

POINTS OF INTEREST:

Greenstead Green – The spire in view for much of this walk is that of St James' Church, designed in the decorative style by G G Scott and built in 1845 on high land between the River Colne and its tributary, Bourne Brook.

Fuschia Nursery – The acres of glasshouses seen when walking down Grange Hill belong to Bakers of Bournebrook Nurseries. They operate a fuschia nursery which enjoys a good reputation and draws many visitors along the little lanes to Greenstead Green.

REFRESHMENTS:

The Hare and Hounds Inn, Greenstead Green.

Maps: OS Sheets Landranger 155, Pathfinder 1029.
The Harvest of the Long Furrow.
Start: At 812378, the lay-by near the red mail box, Audley End.

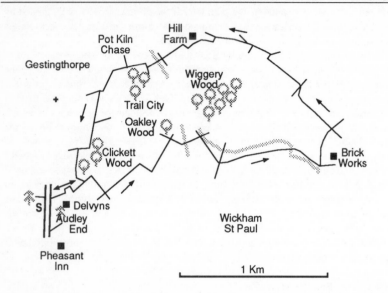

Walk northwards, along the road towards Gestingthorpe, then turn right along Path
19 by the pole at the smaller of Delvyn's gates. Pass a moat, barn, fence and wall to
join the headland towards Clickett Wood. Remember the route taken because you
will be coming back this way and there are no waymarking arrows to show the way.
At the further corner of the wood-cum-pit, fork right on to a headland and, after about
120 yards, turn left along a grassy mid-field path towards Oxley Wood. The path
bends right where the woodland once extended: go left at the next field boundary
junction and approach the present stand of trees on the Wickham St Paul (southern)
side of the boundary ditch.

From the nearest corner of trees, turn right down a re-instated path, go over a
cartbridge, and continue to an unbridged ditch. Go right, moving slightly away from
the ditch to cross a track about 100 yards up from its bridge. Go through a gap in a

hedge to reach a re-instated path pushing up towards **Bulmer's Brick & Tile kiln** and cooling yard. Go over a bridge under an oak tree about 60 yards up from the stream and cut the corner of a smaller field to reach a cartbridge. Cross and turn right, aiming for the thicket in the corner. A walking stick is handy to help find a way through about 10 yards of overgrowth to reach the elbow bend of a bridleway on the Bulmer boundary adjacent to the brickyard.

Go left, uphill, by the cottage, and at the crest, where there is a field opening on the right and a double-hedged bridleway ahead, go left along a mid-field path by a hedge end and walk down to a cartbridge. Cross and climb the headland beyond a ditch end to reach a concrete track at the next crest. Fork left and follow the track to the perimeter of Hill Farm, enjoying fine views of Belchamp Brook valley. Stay to the left of the farm buildings, and from the further garden corner find a re-instated path, by a midfield pole. Dip down to a hand-railed, slatted footbridge. Cross this over the stream feeding Belchamp Brook and climb to the north-east corner of **Trail End Wood**. There, join Pot Kiln Chase along the northern edge of the trees. Stay on Path 8, going left of a pump to enjoy a mown green carpet of welcome at the threshold of Audley End. Off the cut grass, the well-maintained mid-field path climbs the gentle slope, passing to the right of Clickett Wood. At the upper corner, turn right along the headland to Delvyns and retrace the route back to the start.

POINTS OF INTEREST
Bulmer Brick & Tile Kiln – Bricks etc have been produced here continuously since about 1820, using clay from beneath the site. A contract to make land drains during and after the war kept the kilnyard working whilst many others perished. Now specialist bricks for architectural heritage building repairs are made.

Trail End Wood – The wood is at the edge of a permanent site of a camping club with a difference. Their style is cowboy western, and they have developed a thriving community able to welcome passing walkers. There is a path beside the wood, but not through the western-style settlement: entry is by invitation only.

Capt L E G Oates, a very gallant gentleman of Scott's Antarctica Expedition has a memorial in Gestingthorpe church.

REFRESHMENTS
None on the route, but the Pheasant Inn lies just a few yards to the south of the start.

Walk 9   FRINTON-ON-SEA $3^1/_2$m ($5^1/_2$km)

Maps: OS Sheets Landranger 169; Pathfinder 1078 and 1101.

'I do like to be beside the seaside'.

Start: At 242200, Frinton-on-Sea Greensward.

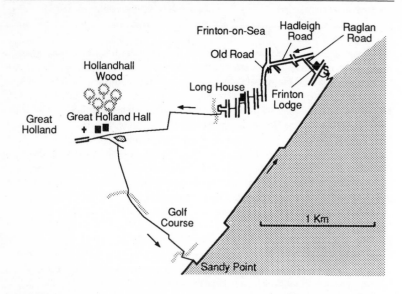

The B1033 road from the west bends south across a level crossing into Frinton-on-Sea and threads its way through Connaught Avenue's shoppers to the Esplanade. There is free parking on the inland edge of the famous Greensward.

Walk north-eastwards as far as Raglan Road by Frinton Lodge. Turn left by Nelmes Cottage, and left again into Hadleigh Road by Ship Cottage. Cross Queen Street and the adjacent Connaught Avenue to reach Old Road. Turn left as far as St Mary Magdalene church. Turn right beyond the church and follow a series of interesting snickets across the meridian road system. First, cross Fourth Avenue, enter a snicket to the right of Summerfield. Cross Third Avenue, bearing slightly left to the next snicket to the left of Long House. Turn left along Second Avenue as far as No. 60, and there turn right into the snicket opposite, descending to First Avenue. Continue the descent into a cul-de-sac to reach a path to the left of No. 10's garden fence. Cross the

22

Kirby Brook footbridge and climb past the tennis court along a mid-field path, heading towards the horizon.

The crenellations of Great Holland's church peep into view, followed by the tree tops of Hollandhall Wood. At the upper level the path bends left and then swings right as a headland to reach Great Holland Hall. Leave all the farm buildings on your right-hand side and turn acutely left around the conservation pond. About 20 yards along Long Lane, fork right on to Short Lane. Follow a mid-field track down to the marshland level. Get to the right-hand side of the dyke, and in the next corner cross a stile on to a golf course. Good links management means that the old footpath is waymarked by black and white marker posts across the fairways, around the greens and tees and over the bridge by a green shelter. Continue along the dyke to reach a concrete cartbridge over Kirby Brook. Mount the seawall steps at Sandy Point and turn left to walk back towards **Frinton-on-Sea**, passing the stilted beach huts known as The Wallings. Go along the front as far as beach hut No. 538, just before the conveniences. Here, ramps and steps climb up the cliff to the greensward by Raglan Road.

POINTS OF INTEREST:
Frinton-on-Sea – In 1881 the population of Frinton was just 55. In 1901 the Frinton Urban Council was formed and a development company under Sir Richard Powell-Cooper set up the seawall and laid out the greensward. Today the town has spread north of the railway line to merge with Walton spreading inland from the Naze. Frinton has a reputation for being a retirement spot, but is also very good for families, the beach being superb.

The most celebrated local sport and social event is the Frinton Tennis Week. Between the two World Wars, when Wimbledon players were not contracted to globe-trotting regimes, many famous names arrived to play with the 'bright set'.

REFRESHMENTS:
The Essex Skipper, Frinton-on-Sea.
There are also numerous other possibilities in the town.

Walk 10   GREAT EASTON AND TILTY   3½m (5½km)

Maps: OS Sheets Landranger 167; Pathfinder 1074 and 1075.

Striding Duton Hill by the Chelmer valley.

Start: At 607255 the car park to the east of the Village Hall, Great Easton.

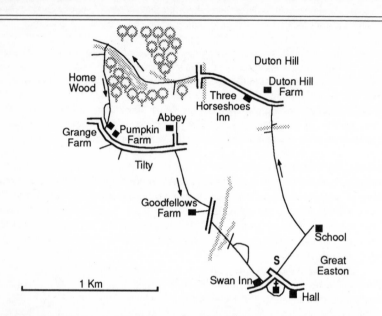

Go through the kissing gate in the car park and walk between the fence posts across the grass. A matching gate gives access to a path beside the school fence. Within the dell another path branches left: follow this mid-field path with soaring views across the Chelmer valley. Cross a slatted bridge and climb along the hedgerow to reach a road opposite Duton Hill Farm. Turn left, passing the Three Horseshoes and the Rising Sun Inns. Descend to the double bridged valley where roads cross both the River Chelmer and the Tilty brook. Cross the former and continue westwards along the northern lip of the deep brook. At the beginning of the woodland, an ivy-clad brick arch bridge swaps the path to the southern lip. Ignore the left turn to the **Abbey**, staying in the valley to go along the wooded brookside and then a hedgerow at the western end of the flood meadow. A complex of waterways provide leat levels for the former

24

Abbey Mill: cross the first of a pair of bridges and go right before the second bridge to walk beside the brook, with the water on your left, around to the northern edge of Home Wood. Another pair of bridges serve the braided stream: this time cross both the brick arch and sleeper forms and then go through a gate and climb the pastured hill, beside the woodland, to reach the top gate. Go through a second, nearby, gate, then pass to the west of a sheepfold and cross a small field to the gap between two barns of Grange Farm.

Follow a short headland around to the concrete drive between the dutch and gabled barns. Turn left along the road by the waymark, passing Pumpkin Farm. The road dips back to the valley of the Chelmer and a mirror on a pole indicates the junction of a lane to Tilty church. After a visit return to the mirrored junction, cross and take the mid-field path opposite, heading down to a bridge over another feeder stream. Great Easton church is now a landmark: aim across the meadow to a pollarded tree by the roadside. Turn right along the road, passing the entrance to Goodfellows Farm, to the right, to reach a kissing gate on the left. Go through and head for the church, crossing a pasture and going over a double handrailed bridge over the Chelmer and the single handrailed bridge of a braided course. One path goes right along the valley, and another continues from the bridges towards the church: wear on the ground suggests the permissive path around the field edges rather than the direct route. Go over a stile in the hedgerow above the convex corner and cross the pasture beyond to reach a stile found by aiming for the church. Follow garden fences to reach **Great Easton** Church green and walk around the churchyard wall to Rebecca Mead and the start.

POINTS OF INTEREST:

Abbey – Tilty Abbey was established in the 12th century, but was mainly destroyed a century later by King John's men following a tax dispute.

Great Easton – The old fort is formed as a mound typical of the Saxon type found in Essex. Located in the grounds of the Hall beside the church, it stands amid Tudor chimneys and by a Norman nave.

REFRESHMENTS:

The Swan Inn, Great Easton.
The Three Horseshoes Inn, Duton Hill.
The Rising Sun Inn, Duton Hill.

Walk 11   STAPLEFORD ABBOTTS $3^1/_2$m ($5^1/_2$km)

Maps: OS Sheets Landranger 167, Pathfinder 1141.
On the Rom-Roding watershed within the motorway's orbit.
Start: At 501961, St Mary's Church, Stapleford Abbotts.

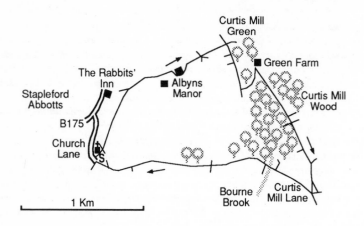

Go through the gate in the churchyard's northern hedge and follow the path beyond across a drive and a grazing slope to reach a stile in the bottom corner, by a large oak tree. Cross and follow the brookside path, to the left, passing a footbridge at the Rabbits' Inn **footpath** junction, to reach a hurdle-cum-stile in the bottom corner. Cross and follow a track up the slope to reach a gate on to Albyns drive. Follow the drive, going to the left of the house towards the clock turret. The way around the multiple barn complex varies with cattle traffic. The best bypass is along the southern side of the clock turret building, where a grassy track which winds towards the lowest building visible in Navestock is reached. Advance to the stile by that cottage. Go over and turn right up Curtis Mill Lane, passing Grafton Farm road and bridging a stream. Just beyond, take the bridleway through the gate on the left, passing between shrubbery and woodland, and curving downhill to reach the green gate of Green Farm.

Coming back uphill from the same gate is another bridleway on a very acute angle – almost an about turn: take this, passing under a canopy of trees and climbing up to the access track for Glade End. Stay west of the U-bend, and at the T-junction of tracks go ahead (southwards) in a slight dip by a corner of the woodland, where Bourne Brook is bridged. Maintain direction to climb beyond the trees, by a bend of overhead wires, continuing to another dwelling's access track. This one merges with upper Curtis Mill Lane at a four-way junction near the parish boundary. Go right, downhill, on the unmade road, crossing a River Rom source stream, and stay on the cinder surface to the green beyond Honeysuckle Cottage.

Go over a stile and follow a hedgeline across several arable fields close to the watershed between the Roding, to the right, and the Rom, to the left, with resultant good views. The right-hand hedge line crosses another path and continues through a gap in the next field, where the hedges thicken to a copse. In the corresponding corner of the second field, cross a headland to reach a plank bridge. The third field has lost its hedged corner, there being a gap from the convex bend to a hedge end. This too is kept on the right-hand side to reach a stile in the high hedging shielding a grazing plot. Go over and follow the left-hand hedge to reach a stile by a trough. Go over on to the upper end of Church Lane. **St Mary's Church** is just a few paces away.

POINTS OF INTEREST

Footpath – Exploring walkers depend upon maps. In the arable countryside of Essex there is no open access: one may walk only on rights-of-way which are highways graded as humble footpaths or greater. To know where the Queen's highways are, maps produced under Crown Copyright are required. Two types of Ordnance Survey maps are used in this book. These are Landranger maps, very useful for armchair planning, for finding the way to the start of a walk, and on the occasions when paths are very visible on the ground, they can be companions actually on a ramble. For navigation, field by field, the Pathfinder map is the real tool to use. It shows field boundaries, past or present and so offers a range of left or right handrails, and other strong clues to follow.

St Mary's Church – Thomas Abdy, an 18th century lawyer, has a memorial in the church. He was a member of a family prominent in Essex for 300 years or more. One of their homes was Albyns, passed on this walk, designed by Inigo Jones. It has housed source material from Sir Thomas Edmondes, very important to historians studying the Elizabethan period.

REFRESHMENTS
The Rabbits' Inn, Stapleford Abbotts.

Walk 12   **WORMINGFORD**   3³/₄m (6km)

Maps: OS Sheets Landranger 168; Pathfinder 1052.

Where St George may have slain a dragon.

Start: At 928317, a lay-by at the top of Sandy Hill (B1508), Wormingford.

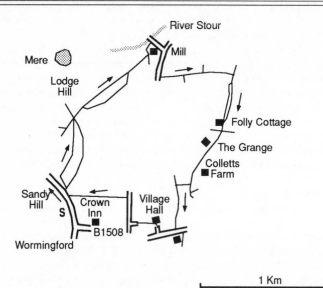

Walk down Sandy Hill to find a couple of stiles 20 yards apart, on the right-hand side. A worn path connects the two on the arable side of the hedge. The path should arc off through the crops, but it is invisiible and rarely used, so take the worn alternative down the inside of the hedge to reach a third stile. Stay beside the fence, walking parallel with the true right of way to Lodge Hill. From the field's gate, cross to a stile on the eastern side of a stand of trees. Do not go over: instead, go right, now with fence on your left, descending into the Stour valley, with a distant viewing of **Wormingford Mere**, surrounded by trees. A gate at the fence end marks the beginning of another diversion. The right of way descends to the Mill via the ditch just beginning on the right-hand side of the field, but common usage is along the established grassy track down to the valley floor. Where the ditch passes under the track, rejoin the proper path by going over the stile to the left. Go right immediately into a triangular pasture and head for the Millhouse. Go over a stile into the garden and walk to the white fencing of the millrace. Follow the drive to the white gate by Wormingford Bridge and the Suffolk border. Stay in Essex by turning right. Bear right at a T-junction, then take the first signed footpath to the left. This oak tree-lined, gravelled track leads past a cottage, then offers views across the Stour to Suffolk. Round the hedge corner at the end of the track, near a very large oak tree, and climb southwards out of the valley.

The path enters a convex corner where the right-hand hedge begins a doubled section: go between the hedgerows, over a stile and follow fences into the field to the left. Stay by the double hedge up the hill to reach Folly Cottage at a cross-paths. Go ahead along Colletts Chase, passing The Grange and Colletts Farm to reach a staggered path crossing by a 'Sound Horn' notice before a bend. Go right up the short track into a field and go left to a corner stile by the three-way junction of triple cables. Now on part of The Hadleigh Way, follow the left field edge to reach the B1508 by Wood Hall. Go right to reach a concrete drive leading to the red brick **Wormingford** village hall, located on a level playing field. Pass along the southern edge of the recreational area to reach Roblett's Way. Turn right along Church Road as far as the footpath signed beyond No 27. Turn left along the path, which offers views of Wormingford Church, to return to the start.

POINTS OF INTEREST:
Wormingford Mere – The Mere, situated beside the River Stour, may have been created by man digging material deposited with the boulder clay at the end of the last Ice Age. Road making always demands hoggin, for example, or impervious clay was needed to staunch the Stour. Local legend has it that the Mere is both bottomless and haunted. Furthermore Sir George de la Haye is believed to have slain a dragon on its banks. The scene is depicted in stained glass in a northern window of St. Andrew's church. Was this St George ?
Wormingford – Peacefully soaring over the walker's head may be another set of quiet recreation-seekers: members of the Essex & Suffolk Gliding Club. Their base is on part of the former World War II Wormingford Airfield used mainly for USAAF operations, as may be noted from the memorials at Wormingford Green and in the church.

REFRESHMENTS:
The Crown, Wormingford.

RADWINTER 3³/₄m (6km)

Maps: OS Sheets Landranger 154; Pathfinder 1050 and 1051.
From riverside, across a Roman road and back to riverside.
Start: At 609373, the lay-by near the Pant bridge, Radwinter.

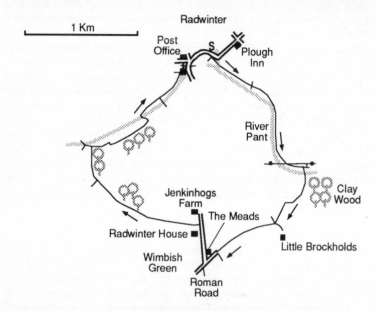

Opposite the lay-by, by the AWA pump compound, there is a stile into a meadow: go over and cross to the field's south-east corner to a footbridge over the brook. Now riverside, walk downstream, going over a stile to reach another by the concrete slab bridge. Cross and follow a wide arable headland beside the **River Pant** as far as a girder bridge. Now stay left of the river through further grazing fields to reach arable land again. A line of poles converge with the riverside path and a thorn thicket grows under the cables: go right of the thicket to reach a footbridge. South of the Pant, cross the narrow neck of a field to the hedge end and walk up the valley, separated from Clay Wood by a narrow belt of grassland. The left-hand hedge bows right towards Mortlocks Farm: at a bend in the hedge, go left, to reach a path junction beyond the old defence blockhouse. Go left by the yellow marker for a few paces, then swing right, downhill, along the drive from Little Brockholds, climbing to reach the Roman road by The Meads. Turn right, away from **Wimbish Green**, passing Radwinter House and Springfield to reach Path 34, which begins by some rounded wartime huts on the left. Join a path by the silver fir tree west of the huts and follow it along the hedge to the right. Step over the ditch above Jenkinhogs Farm and follow a lovely field-edge path across several fields, gently returning to the Pant valley. Further down the valley several ditches are crossed by sleeper bridges as the path descends to reach a second wood on the right-hand side.

Go over a plank bridge into the field below the northern edge of this stand of trees. Turn right and when beyond the wood, go over a cartbridge to get to the upper level. Now follow the field boundary ENE, passing a newly planted belt of trees. At the far end of the plantation, turn left with the ditch bend, then go left again over a bridge. Almost immediately a brick arch bridge offers a right turn over the Pant: take it, then go right again over a third bridge and walk downstream, by an extended bridge, to pass between river and railings towards the church. The railings bend left: follow a path across a water meadow and up a gentle slope to the gated bridge by the brick and flint walls around St Mary the Virgin Church. The south porch has an upper storey and on the other side of the churchyard is the pargetted post office by one of the cross-roads in Radwinter. Turn along the B1053 towards Sampford to return to the brookside lay-by.

POINTS OF INTEREST:

River Pant – The rivers Pant, Roding, Bourne, Cam, Can, Colne, Chelmer and the Stour-feeding Bumpstead Brook all rise within a few miles of this part of Essex. The Bourne joins the Granta and together they flow in to the Cam en route to the Wash. The Roding is bound for the Thames at Barking Creek. The Can joins the Chelmer at Chelmsford and together they make an estuary at Maldon shared with the Blackwater which, in its upper reaches, was called the Pant.

Wimbish Green – Drainage to enhance agriculture has exercised minds here as elsewhere. Thomas Tusser was advocating new schemes at Wimbish Green in 1557. Brushwood drains between *stetches* – strips of land nearly 3 yards wide – were tried. Steam-driven ploughing machines in the 19th century were also tried. Perhaps the most radical method was to lay straw ropes in hollow drains set in a radial pattern from the centre of the field.

REFRESHMENTS:
The Plough Inn, Radwinter.

Walk 14   BELHUS LAKESIDE BEAT $3\frac{3}{4}$m (6km)

Maps: OS Sheets Landranger 177; Pathfinder 1160.
Adventure in Upminster country.
Start: At 565826, Belhus Woods Country Park, Aveley.

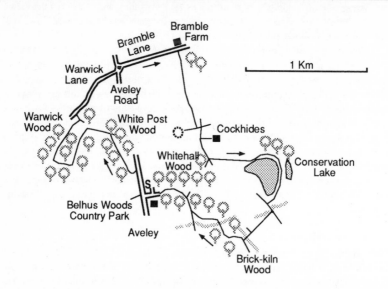

Head north-westwards from the Information Centre to use the permissive path inside
Aveley Road hedge to reach a road. Cross into the south-east corner of White Post
Wood. Walk the perimeter path clockwise to the opposite corner exit, straddled by a
pylon. Follow a headland across to Warwick Wood and repeat the clockwise perimeter
walk. Along the southern edge a broader path begins: follow it NNE through the trees
to its end, then turn left to Warwick Lane. Turn right to reach a junction with Aveley
Road. Cross into Bramble Lane, following it as far as Bramble Farm. Turn right over
a stile into a reclaimed pit site. Follow the left-hand fenceline to a slatted bridge. A
vast grassland stretches southward: head for the **Queen Elizabeth II bridge** at first,
then as the sandy spoilheaps loom nearer, nudge left a little to converge with Cockhide's
track. Cross another slatted bridge to reach a quarry road. Go left for 10 yards, then
right for 150 yards to reach a track bend, re-entering the Country Park. Now follow a

wood-chip path between green metal gates, with Whitehall Wood to the right. Opposite a path, right, signed 'Path 265 to Path 264' is a wooden footbridge. Cross this to open grassland and head eastwards for Conservation Lake. Go clockwise around the water, using a narrow sandy path by the northern fence and then rounding to a causeway by a smaller lake to the left.

To the south of the large lake, by an ancient hedgerow, turn left, away from the water, towards a cartbridged gate and kissing stile over Running Water Brook. Go through the gate, turn right and leave the brook south-westwards along a path. Go past the northern end of a vestigal oaken hedgerow, cross an unmown pipeline strip and head for a gate by the south-east corner of Brick-kiln Wood. Join a bridleway where it swaps sides of Long Pond's brook. Cross a bridge and immediately go right under the woodland canopy. A path serpentines westwards to reach another bridleway. Turn right through the trees to re-cross Running Water Brook. Turn left immediately after crossing a bridge, going along a stone-hardened narrow path to a small clearing. Left is a charming boardwalk over an Aesop mirror: get to the path west of it and walk northwards on Path 264, later swinging westwards on Path 263 to return to the start.

POINTS OF INTEREST:
Queen Elizabeth II bridge – Grays Thurrock, to the south of the walk, was home to 33 families in 1723. The increasing trend of population through migration was evident in 1801 when 113 families lived there. St Peter's and St Paul's church dates from 1846, and Tilbury docks from 1886. Now the reputation for heavy industry in this vast urban area is beginning to shift towards fame for service industries. The London orbital road, Dartford Tunnel and Queen Elizabeth II Bridge are examples. Outdoor facilities other than Belhus Woods Country Park, are found at Stubbers, Mar Dyke Way, the Chase Forest, with communal projects in Stifford, Chafford Hundred and much more.

REFRESHMENTS:
Available at the Belhus Woods Park Information Centre, though this has limited opening.
There are also several possibilities in Aveley.

Walk 15   DEBDEN AND WIDDINGTON   3³/₄m (6km)

Maps: OS Sheets Landranger 167; Pathfinder 1050.
Field path links for two fine Essex churches.
Start: At 555336, the car park by the village pond, Debden.

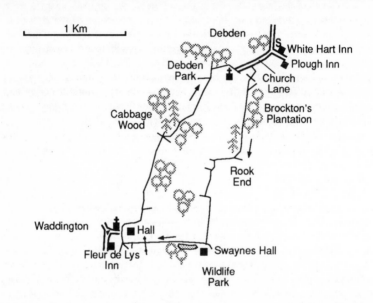

This short walk is rich with interest. It detains the walker and defies an overall pace
beyond a dawdle. Start with a charming descent towards St Mary the Virgin and All
Saints' Church. Pass New Cottage and Old Cottage to reach a stile by Park House. Go
over and take Path 42 which branches off beside Old Cottage garden, bending right
by the field boundary towards the brick arboretum wall. Cross a waymarked footbridge
to the path to the eastern side of the stream. Head southwards by Brocton's Plantation
and Spinney Wood to reach a double-stiled bridge one small field away from Rook
End. Cross the field beyond diagonally to reach Rook End Lane. Turn right, then fork
left of the thatched cottages and a byway. As the track bends right to Dunstable's
barn, go ahead, uphill, along the field edge to reach a crossditch. Turn left and round
a hedge corner to resume a southwards route. Go uphill to Swaynes Hall cross-paths.

34

Turn right passing to the north of a moat and woodland. From the north-west corner of the trees a mid-field path heads westwards to a restored, converted barn. Aim for the cable-carrying pole which appears to be one space south of the pole by the church. In fact, when the path passes under the wires, and the hedge-side path by the barn is clearly in view. Stay field-side of the barn's hedge and in the north-west corner go under the thicket cover to reach a bend of Church Street, **Widdington**. Turn right to the church. The route continues along the right side of the church, along Path 4. Bend right along the northern side of Dovehouse Close, and from the hedge corner follow a mid-field green strip northwards. At a mid-field ditch source, the path bends right with the ditch, and the required path continues ahead, downhill, to the south-west corner of the woodland. Go over a footbridge and follow the left edge of Park Wood. Cross a large field towards two byres at the southern edge of Cabbage Wood. Pass between the two buildings, veering right to a stile on to a track that threads through the trees to reach a fine view across the valley to Debden Park. Now aim for a red-brick building, cross a bridge and turn right, following the railings back by the church. Go up Church Lane to return to the start in **Debden**.

POINTS OF INTEREST:

Widdington – Priors Hall Barn, west of the church, is a magnificent 15th-century agricultural building open on certain summer weekends. Priors Hall, Swaynes Hall and Mole Hall, all close to the village, are fine examples of grand farmhouses. The Mole Hall Wildlife Park, to the south of Swaynes Hall, is a popular destination for family excursions because of the care and concern shown to resident wildlife and visiting humans. Native and foreign animals are on display, and there is a notable area for butterflies to flutter by. There is a playground, a nature trail, an insect house and a guinea pig run.

Debden – There are two villages named Debden in Essex, one close to Epping Forest and this one. This is the Debden that won a national Village Ventures Award in 1982/3 in recognition of initiatives and innovations shown by the local community for Rural Voice concerns.

REFRESHMENTS:

The White Hart, Debden.
The Plough, Debden.
The Fleur de Lys, High Street, Widdington.

Maps: OS Sheets Landranger 154 and 167; Pathfinder 1050.

A mainstream Essex parish for walking.

Start: At 481356, the lay-by at a road junction near Newland End, north of Arkesden.

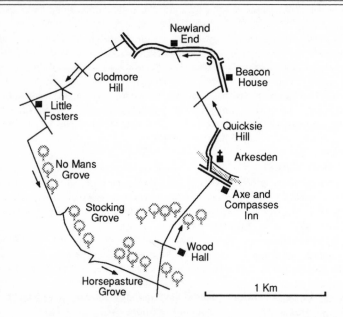

Walk westwards, passing neat Newland End Farm, to reach a T-junction by a red letterbox in Wicken Water valley. Turn right, for Duddenhoe End, then left by the thatched cottages on a lane signed for Clodmore Hill. Ford or footbridge Wicken Water and follow the lane up the ridge beyond Clodmore Hill Farm to a three-way junction by Little Fosters. Ignore Bull Green Lane, to the right, and Stevens Lane, to the left, to follow the cleared bridleway passing to the right of the dwelling. When you reach a small transformer on a pole south of the chicken run, turn left and follow a field-edge path along the northern and eastern boundaries of the field to reach a junction above Clavering Farm. Turn left along the **ridge**, using field-edge paths which vary in texture as they trace the woodlands of No Man's Grove below Mill Mound.

Jockey left-right over bridges to reach the edge of Stocking Grove, then manoeuvre right-left to traverse the southern face of Horsepasture Grove.

Another track follows the hedge up from Stickling Green and crosses the ridge. Turn left where overhead wires slant across the next field to share a gap in the trees cut by the track. Follow the track to a white wooden cottage, then continue northwards along field-edge paths, off the ridge. Go across the track in the next covert, and head down towards the church in Wicken Water valley, reaching a road by a sub-station. Turn right to the **Axe and Compasses Inn**. Go over the bridge by the inn and turn left, to be still separated from the road by a stream. Turn right along the road, going around the bend by the pump, seats and Jubilee Oak, then climbing, via the churchyard, up Quicksie Hill. By the end of the hedge on the left-hand side of the road, a signed path goes left. Follow this along a field edge, then, beyond the hedge corner, follow a glorious mid-field path towards Newland End. At a cross-paths, turn right along another mid-field path heading for the right-hand side of Beacon House to reach a road. Turn left to return to the lay-by.

POINTS OF INTEREST:
Ridge – The ridge walk alongside No Man's, Stocking and Horsepasture Groves is close to a watershed. The valley in view, containing several fishponds, drains in to the River Stort which is Thames-bound. The valley just forded en route to the ridge, and to which the walk returns from Wood Hall, contains Wicken Water, a tributary of the River Cam which is Wash-bound. The contours of Essex are not prolific, but the drainage pattern obeys them still!
Axe and Compasses Inn – This is a very picturesque, 17th-century thatched pub. Superbly set amid similarly charming buildings clustered by Wicken Water, it completes the picture below St Mary the Virgin's sturdy church dating from the 13th century. It is a popular pub, offering good food, fine ale and a collection of interesting and amusing artifacts.

REFRESHMENTS:
The Axe and Compasses Inn, Arkesden.

Walk 17   EAST MERSEA   4m (6¹/₂km)

Maps: OS Sheets Landranger 168; Pathfinder 1100.
Island enchantment amid a National Nature Reserve.
Start: At 066147, Cudmore Grove Country Park.

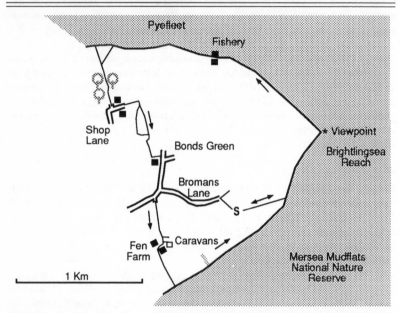

The Park lies about 4 miles off the B1025. Fork left for East Mersea off The Strood causeway on to the island and follow East Road to reach Country Park signs which point along to the end of Bromans Lane.

Check the high tide time at the Information Centre: part of this walk is along the Groves eroded foreshore, and it is unusable at some high tides. Allow about twelve minutes to walk the foreshore and avoid it one hour either side of high tide time. As the entire walk takes almost two hours to complete, a reversal of direction should make this walk possible at any time.

Head eastwards across the park to reach a stile where the shallow cliff of the grove gives way to a borrow dyke behind a seawall. Move up the Colne estuary wall to the stepping-stones to a favourite viewing point on a shingle bank. Across Brightlingsea Reach the view includes the opening of Flag Creek flanked by

38

Brightlingsea's Batemans Tower and Point Clears Martello Tower. Regain the seawall path and continue along the elevated route, punctuated by stiles, keeping a watch for **shipping** and **wildlife**. Near the opening to Pyefleet Channel is a fishery farm operating on both sides of the wall. Soon after, at 054158, turn left and cross a bridge over the borrow dyke into a field. Follow the fence to a stile at the northern end of a grove. Go over on to a path which threads through the narrow belt of trees to a stile. Continue on a short lane passing The Saltings to reach Shop Lane.

Turn left by Dowsing, and from the end of Shop Lane take a path towards North Farm. Another path joins it immediately beyond High Hoe: use this path to continue the shallow climb away from the estuary to a hedge corner. Follow the left-hand hedge in the upper field, bearing left with the path as it becomes a green lane to Bonds Green. Join East Road to pass The Anchorage, right, and face any oncoming traffic beyond the Bromans Lane junction. Turn next left on a drive to Fen Farm caravan park. Pass the west side of the farmhouse to reach a grassy track descending gently to the beach of the Mersea Mudflats Nature Reserve. Turn left along the foreshore, crossing a stream to reach 065144. From here 12 minutes should be available for a safe passage beneath the low cliff of Cudmore Grove. If not, take a short cut directly up to the Park. On the beach, continue until the ramp up to the Park is reached. Now retrace the outward route back to the start.

POINTS OF INTEREST:
Shipping – Mersea Island watches over a double estuary. East Mersea is by the Colne shipping lanes to Colchester, Rowhedge, Wivenhoe and Brightlingsea. Movement is restricted to high water, and pilots frequently anchor in Brightlingsea Reach awaiting the moment to go upstream. The larger estuary of the Blackwater carries the least traffic now Maldon, Heybridge, Maylandsea and Tollesbury all have more recreational than commercial craft. Empty ocean-going vessels sometimes ride high at anchor off Bradwell, awaiting their next commissions.

Wildlife – The great drowned coastal valleys of Essex are like tidal lakes, revealing, at each low tide, a rich meal table for hundreds of migrating wader-birds. The Colne Estuary National Nature Conservancy monitor the happenings in this muddy wilderness.

REFRESHMENTS:
The Dog & Pheasant, East Mersea is along East Road on the way off the island.
The Rose, Peldon is conveniently situated on the mainland side of The Strood .
Cudmore Grove Country Park has a splendid picnic area and coffee vending.

Walk 18 WRABNESS 4m (6½km)

Maps: OS Sheets Landranger 169; Pathfinder 1053.
Beside a beautiful East Anglian Estuary.
Start: At 174319 , Church Road, Wrabness.

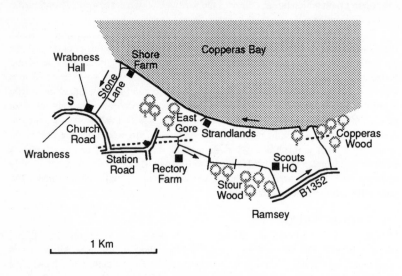

Walk eastwards along panoramic Church Road, turning left along Station Road and
left again by the station. Now follow Black Boy Lane over the **railway** bridge and
immediately turn right to walk beside the railway fence to the next bridge. Cross back
to the southern side and turn left by a pond to follow a path heading ESE across a field
to reach the woodland fringe. Go over a double stile on to a woodland path, maintaining
direction to reach a dwelling beside a track. Now take the path heading eastwards,
going through habitats created to encourage butterflies. Maintain the easterly direction
through **Stour Wood**, sometimes on a waymarked path, sometimes not, until the Scout
headquarters are located on the eastern edge of the woodland. Turn right, still under
the trees, to reach the B1352. Turn left, with care, to reach the entrance to Copperas
Wood. Go left along a track, bearing left at the fork to cross a railway bridge. The
track descends to public hides (courtesy of the RSPB) overlooking Copperas Bay:

continue along the edge of the Bay, heading westwards along a mown path and then along a field edge to reach Strandlands.

Continue over several stiles and bridges, passing a private jetty and hide, and then going through East Gore spinney. The path is by trees on the very fringe of the bay, some of the trees having toppled to a salty decay, whilst others hang on with a partial root system. As Shore Farm is approached, the path mounts the protective seawall, winding through the tamarisk shrubs. Now from a point near where the saltings give way to the beach, follow Stone Lane, to the left, uphill, passing Wrabness Hall to reach a road junction. Turn right back to the start.

POINTS OF INTEREST:

Railway – The track is a branch line from Manningtree to Harwich. It is also the European link from Ipswich and London, Liverpool Street to Parkeston Quay. Wrabness Station, when it had a live-in station master was a frequent winner of the annual station garden competitions. Set in a sun-trap cutting, the cleverly attended flower beds were worth a train journey to see.

Stour Wood – The wood is owned by the Woodland Trust and managed by the Royal Society for the Protection of Birds. There are permissive paths in addition to the public paths and they, and the information board, are appreciated by many visitors annually. The hide overlooking Copperas Bay is particularly popular, and its wall charts have helped many people identify the graceful probers of the mudflats.

REFRESHMENTS:

The Black Boy, Wrabness.
The Wheatsheaf, on the B1352.
The Castle Inn, Ramsey, on the B1352.

Walks 19 & 20 MISTLEY THORN AND MISTLEY HEATH 4m (6$\frac{1}{2}$km) or 6m (9$\frac{1}{2}$km)

Maps: OS Sheets Landranger 169; Pathfinder 1053.

Where seaborne and seashore activities interlock.

Start: At 104320, Riverside East Fiveways car park, Manningtree.

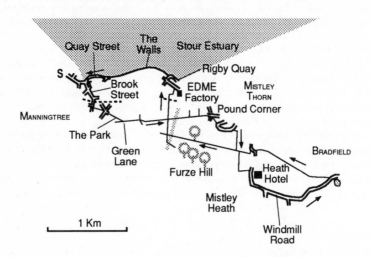

Leave the car park beside the Inn and cross to the market place by the village sign. Go right up Brook Street by the Swan Inn, bear right to cross the railway bridge and turn left by the Evangelical Church on to a path to cross New Street by the Waggon and Horses Inn. Go through The Park to reach a path from Park bungalow's gate. Follow this to Green Lane. Go left: the lane dips and rises, becoming Shrubland Road and reaching the B1352 at Pound Corner. Turn right along a path to Middlefield Road and Rigby Avenue. Around the crescent is a small green. Take the path heading south by bungalow No. 31, going under wires to reach a path junction at a pole with strainers.

The shorter route turns right here. The longer route turns left, returning to this junction to follow the shorter route back to the start.

Turn left, then right over a stile. Head south, then turn left to reach the blue garage of a cottage. Go over a stile on to a road and turn right along Windmill Road, passing the Heath Hotel. Ignore turnings to the right, following the road (which becomes Mill Lane) to a wooded bend by the pond. Here, a waymark points left up a field to a crossing place in the kink of the western hedge, where the path merges with overhead wires. Cross the next field, passing irrigation points (a good example of land husbandry linking an old highway with modern needs) to reach a lagoon in a railway cutting. The line, intended to cross the plain of Tendring was not completed. A causeway leads to a field: follow the left-hand hedge to reach a road bend by a dwelling 'Wymark'. Nearby is the ruin of St Mary's Church, Mistley Heath, now replaced by a church nearer The Towers. Bear right, but leave the road at the next bend, turning left towards Church Farm. Go right before the ecclesiastical windows, pass north of a barn to rejoin the shorter walk at the path junction.

Head west along a field edge path, passing a recreation ground, to the right, then descending through the woodland of Furze Hill. Go over a stile beyond a lake into a field, continuing down to a bridge. Cross to reach a path junction. Turn right, crossing rough fields linked by stiles and crossing the lane walked on the outward route. Continue past School Wood, on the right, heading for the arch in the railway embankment. Go through, cross a footbridge and turn right by a silo to enter the aromatic factory yard of **EDME**. Be alert for forklift trucks etc., keeping to the right of way to reach High Street. Turn left to the ornamental swan by the craft centre at **Rigby Quay**. Now, west of the weighbridge, a short path links the north side of Robert Adams' twin towers to The Walls. Go over Hopping Bridge and walk back to Manningtree. Fork right on to Quay Street, following it to North Street and High Street by the market place. To the right is the Skinners Arms: the car park is behind it.

POINTS OF INTEREST:

EDME – Thomas Tusser (1515-1580), the author of Five Hundred Points of Good Husbandry, introduced the growing of barley to this area. It has been a successful crop, as the EDME (English Diastatic Malt Extract) factory testifies.

Rigby Quay – Named for Richard Rigby and his son, who successively developed Mistley Thorn as a spa town founded upon local industry and craft.

REFRESHMENTS:
The Skinners Arms, Manningtree.
The Swan Inn, Manningtree.
The Waggon & Horses Inn, Mistley.

Walk 21   SILVER END AND WHITE NOTLEY   4m (6½km)

Maps: OS Sheets Landranger 167 and 168; Pathfinder 1075, 1098 and 1099.

On the flank of the River Brain by Cressing Temple Barns.
Start: At 801193, Temple Lane, Silver End.

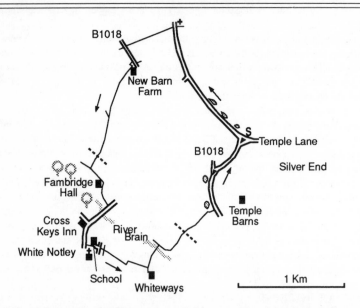

There is ample opportunity for temporary parking near the triangular junction.

Walk north-eastwards along Church Road towards Cressing, turning left along a waymarked path as the All Saints' Church, with its stunted belfry is approached. Follow it across fields to reach the B1018. Turn left along the footway as far as the second waymark on the right. Enter a field and within a few paces swap sides of a ditch. A headland now stretches south-westwards, offering views of arable fields and wooded patches in a folded landscape. The headland steepens as it enters the River Brain valley: pass under an arch carrying the Witham-Braintree railway and turn left at a T-junction of tracks. Climb to Fambridge Hall and fork right to join Station Road in White Notley. Turn right, crossing the river into the charming village centre by the Cross Keys Inn. Go up Church Hill towards Faulkbourne and enter the churchyard.

Several cut grass paths criss-cross amid the headstones: select the south-east exit by the school fence, and follow its drive to Vicarage Avenue.

The path continues beside house No. 30, by the transformer on a pole. Enter the field behind the gardens and follow the left-hand hedge through two fields to the corner steps by Whiteways. Go left, away from the buildings, following the left-hand boundaries down to a footbridge over the River Brain. Turn right along the riverbank as far as a field corner, and then follow the right-hand hedge up the valley side to reach a double-stiled crossing of the railway. Cross, with great care, and continue along the right-hand hedge to reach ponds and the B1018, swapping to the southern side of the hedge for the last few yards. Opposite is the site of **Temple Barns**. Turn left along the B1018 to its junction with Temple Lane. Go right to return to the starting triangle near **Silver End**.

POINTS OF INTEREST:

Temple Barns – From 1135 Cressing Manor was a training ground for the Knights Templar. King Stephen granted 600 acres of Cressing to the Order in 1150. There were probably another dozen such training grounds in England at the time. The Knights Templar were responsible for the safety of pilgrims to the Holy Land then dominated by Moslems who saw pilgrim tourists as objects for extortion and robbery. The Templars owed allegiance to no one except the Pope – a position of power which they exploited as well as they fought. This position excited envy and 200 years later the Holy Inquisition toppled them. The Cressing estate was transferred, in the 14th century, to the Hospitalers, the Knights of St John who had responsibility for nursing the wounded. They held the estate until the Dissolution of the monasteries. Both the weatherboarded and the brick-built barns are thought to be at least 12th century buildings.

Silver End – Frank Crittall, after some experience in the machine shops of the Black Country, found himself proprietor of an ironmongery in Braintree at the age of 22. He designed metal window frames and set up a manufacturing and galvanising plant by Rivenhall. Around the works he and his family designed and created a new village – Silver End.

REFRESHMENTS:
The Cross Keys Inn, White Notley.
The Western Arms, Silver End.
The Silver End Hotel, Silver End.

Walk 22   **GREAT TOTHAM**   4m (6½km)

Maps: OS Sheets Landranger 168; Pathfinder 1099.
A Walk in Spickets gravel countryside.
Start: At 857114, School Road, Great Totham.

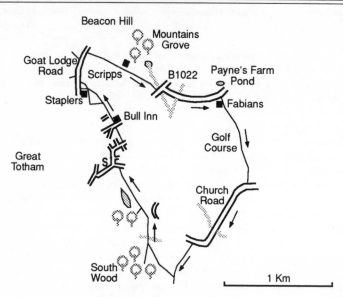

Walk north-eastwards along **School Road** and turn left along Hall Road. Turn into the second cul-de-sac on the right, then go along the snicket by No. 12 (Seagers). Turn left before a barricade to reach a fine cricket field commanding extensive views. Follow the path to the B1022, cross, with care, and follow the path to the left of the Bull Inn into a field. Cross to the sycamores in the north-west corner, then follow the cottage drive to Staplers to reach a road. Turn right along bracken-lined **Goat Lodge Road,** passing two paths to the left, before turning right opposite Little Hill's gate. Enjoy the views from around Scripps Farm as the drive is followed under the wires to the B1022. Turn left, then cross, with care, into Beckingham Road, on the right. Follow the road over Spickets Brook, walking towards Totham Hill Green as far as Payne's Farm pond. Now ignore the path by Angham House in preference for one waymarked along the eastern side of Fabians Farm. In a corner by a disused gateway to the golf course, bear left between a fence and a hedge, going along the non-golf side. In the next corner go over a double plank bridge into a field. A larger bridge gives access to another field. Cross this to a road.

Turn right along Church Road, going around a sharp right bend. Soon after, turn left along a stony lane, following it south-westwards to a point where wires pass over the hedgerow. A footbridge straddles Catchpole Brook nearby: cross it and the field beyond to the tentative corner of South Wood. Path 18 continues across the field to another footbridge, but local usage has worn a diversion along the woodland edge to join Path 31, to make a shorter crossing of the field. Cross the bridge and the next field, on a grassy strip, to enter the churchyard. Go through a kissing gate on the far side of St Peter's Church, following Path 18 past the moat, the red-brick wall, and other buildings of Great Totham Hall, on the right. Now follow the fencing beside residential barns (in an area once renowned for Gilbert Kemsley's prize-winning gilt pigs) to reach an avenue of lime trees bordering a pitscape developed from a former gravel extraction zone. At the top of the avenue a door-sized kissing gate gives access to the former Pound Field, now a construction yard. Pass through, with caution, following the right-hand fencing to reach a similar tall gate and, beyond, a stile on to Hall Road. Go left, then left again into School Road.

POINTS OF INTEREST:

School Road – Nestling around a courtyard in School Road are the Willie Almshouses. Built in 1855 by William and Louisa Gooday, the courtyard is complete with a small chapel, a bellcote and clocktower.

Goat Lodge Road – The upper end of Goat Lodge Road is known as Beacon Hill. A beacon was lit there in 1988 to celebrate the Armada dealings of 1588. Nearby are Mountains Farm and Mountains Grove: the area has been charmingly dubbed Essex Mountain.

REFRESHMENTS:

The Bull Inn, Great Totham.
The Prince of Wales, Great Totham.

Walk 23   CLACTON-ON-SEA   4m (6½km)

Maps: OS Sheets Landranger 168; Pathfinder 1101.

Golden sands on the sunshine coast.

Start: At 176145, Pier Gap, Clacton-on-Sea.

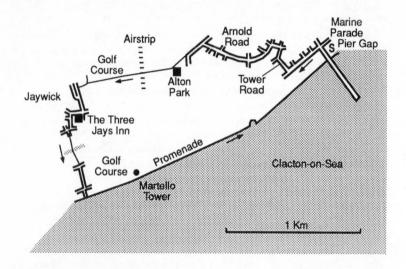

From Pier Gap, walk three sunken gardens westwards to the pedestrian crossing over Marine Parade West. Turn right by the Martello tower with the observers' hut on top, and walk Tower Road, forking right by the Theatre. Round the corner by St James' Church, and go left along Wash Lane. Fork left to Arnold Road, following it to its T-junction with Leas Road at the flat topped St Monicas's Court. Turn left, but where the road bears left to Cherry Tree Avenue, go ahead along a path through fields. Go past Alton Park Farm, following Path 15 over a stile on to an airstrip. Cross, with care, looking both ways, but especially right, and listening. Go past a lovely pitscape, to the left, then follow a track past Millers Barn golf course to join **Jaywick Lane**. Turn left to a double roundabout by the Three Jays Inn. Turn right to reach Union Road, behind the inn. Go right along Crossways, then turn left through the gap between Nos. 9 and 17. Follow a path across an open playing space to Jasmine

Way. Go straight ahead, along Garden Road to reach Golf Green Road. Opposite and slightly right is Badminton Road: follow it to reach steps up to the Promenade.

Tendring District Council attracts tourists with the slogan 'The Sunshine Coast'. It does rain here, but only just over an inch per month on average, less than most other resorts in the country. Less rain means less clouds means more sun.

Turn left along the Promenade, passing the end of the housing to reach a Martello tower, one of the 114 ranged around the coast as a defence against Napoleon's expected invasion. The walk now passes a golf course and a lagoon to reach a new housing estate which occupies the site of Butlins Holiday Park where many people gained fond memories of **Clacton-on-Sea**. Go around the Water Sports ramp and pass the Winston Churchill plaque, enjoying the murals by Simon Barber on your way back to Pier Gap.

POINTS OF INTEREST:

Jaywick Lane – A narrow gauge railway opened in Jaywick during the summer of 1936, sponsored by the Jaywick Estates. It ran from Jaywick Sands along an old seawall, through a tunnel, across marshland to Crossways station where water and coal was stored. The service was half-hourly during summer months. Alas, the track was requisitioned for coastal defences in 1939 and the rails were taken as scrap iron for the war effort. The engine went to another narrow gauge line in Scotland and the rolling stock found a home on Cumbria's Eskdale Railway.

Clacton-on-Sea – Clactonian Man inhabited one of the earliest known sites of human occupation on these isles, so early he may have walked from France before the creation of the Dover Straits. However, the pioneer of modern Clacton-on-Sea was Peter Schuyler Bruff. Born 23rd July 1812 he became a civil engineer assisting with the construction of the Eastern Union Railway to Colchester, completed in 1843. When exploring the land beyond Colchester he recognised the potential of the coast and set about developing the resort we see today. He built Clacton Pier in 1871 to bring in building supplies with a view to landing holiday-makers there later. He was a churchman, a yachtsman, a good raconteur, and he lived to his eighty-ninth year.

REFRESHMENTS:

The Three Jays Inn, on the route.

In addition, items to chew, munch, lick or sip are available at frequent intervals in Clacton-on-Sea and Jaywick.

Walk 24   PENTLOW AND FOXEARTH   4m (6¹/₂km)

Maps: OS Sheets Landranger 155, Pathfinder 1029.
The Stour valley, looking at Gainsborough's country.
Start: At 832464, just off the A1092 near Foxearth.

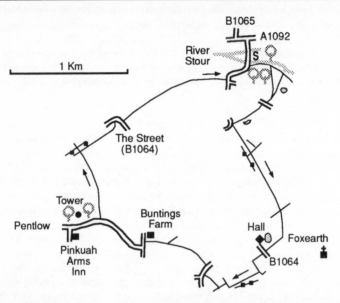

Between Cavendish and Long Melford on the A1092, about 200 yards after the B1065 goes left, to Glemsford, there is a turn to the right for Foxearth. This road dips to two bridges over courses of the river Stour at the county boundary. On the island between the bridges is a large lay-by used by anglers, and ramblers alike.

Cross the southern bridge and turn left to walk the river bank, with a pitscape on your right-hand side. Fencing impels the path to stay riverside a little further than the map shows, as far as a fallen tree, the bole of which makes a clumsy stile to grassland. The path splits in two here: take the southern fork, passing to the right of a pond and continuing to a road. Go right for some 30 yards, then turn left along a path up the left-hand, wide hedgerow of a field to reach a road at a bend. Another path also reaches the bend: use this, following overhead wires as far as the second cross-paths. Here, go left through a hole in the hedge and continue down the eastern side of the same hedgerow to reach a footbridge and stile in the corner. Cross and take three or four paces across a narrow neck of meadow to reach a double stiled footbridge to another meadow. Walk by the left-hand hedge as far as a pole, then cross mid-field, westwards, with good views of the moat, to reach a stile by a garden corner.

Go through the remaining plot along the left-hand hedge to reach the B1064 in **Foxearth**. Opposite and to the left is a continuation path by another garden hedge. Go through a thicket, cross a footbridge and follow the field boundary headland to the far south-west corner. Turn north for a few paces to reach a single plank bridge, to the left, hard by a junction of ditches. Go over, then cross the second ditch by cartbridge and proceed mid-field towards the cottage over the road. Turn right along the road, then go left along the re-instated path from the cottage's garden corner, heading north-westwards, mid-field, to reach a gap in a bend of the hedgerow to the east of Buntings Farm. Cross the field beyond to a stile to the left of the farm. Go over and cross to a gate on to a road. Go left, and right at the road junction. Follow the road to reach Hoe Lane, to the right: the Pinkuah Arms Inn is just ahead. Turn down Hoe Lane, at the base of the **Tower**, following it to a point where there is a reservoir, left, a field boundary, right, and wires overhead. There, turn right and walk along the field edge towards the bottom of Pentlow Hill, where a small settlement is known as Pentlow Street. When you are about 70 yards short of the buildings, swing left, following wheelmarks across to a black barn and a road (B1064). Turn right, with care, to reach a signed bridleway to the left. Turn along this green lane, which is sometimes damp in places. It improves as it swings gently right and climbs away from the undercutting River Stour. Dip equally gently – the bridleway is a headland for one stretch – to reach a T-junction of roads. Turn left and follow the road back to the start.

POINTS OF INTEREST

Foxearth – St Peter's & St Paul's is an ornate Victorian church with much interior decoration and knapped flintwork outside. An avenue of lime trees keeps the churchyard secluded from vehicular interruption. The adjacent primary school is frequently attractive with the potential for pupil activity. The porch, even on a Sunday, is usually aligned with tiny colourful wellies, perhaps ready for Monday's pond dipping.
Tower – Bull's or Rectory Tower, or Pentlow Folly as it is also known, was built in 1858 by Rector Edward Bull in memory of his father. That it is a tall and thin building can be ascertained from many miles distant, but a closer view is denied by foliage on private property around the base. It is said to be an irregular polygon in plan.

REFRESHMENTS
The Pinkuah Arms, Pentlow, just off the route.

Maps: OS Sheets Landranger 167; Pathfinder 1050.
Tree-lined paths over a rolling, rounded landscape.
Start: At 512336, a lay-by near St Helen's Chapel, Newport.

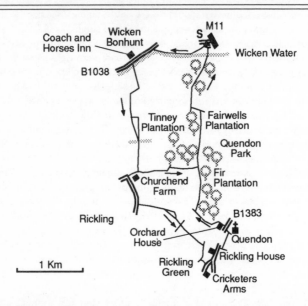

Walk to the western end of the lay-by and turn left along a signed path heading south-westwards to Wicken Water. Turn right to follow the brook upstream to reach the B1038. Turn left into Wicken Bonhunt. Opposite the Coach and Horses Inn, between two dwellings, a track heads southwards. Take this, crossing a bridge and climbing out of the valley to the site of the former Rectory Wood. Cross the upper bridge, and go right to follow a headland around a corner, continuing uphill and transfering to the western side of the hedgerow. The map shows the track heading straight for Rickling Churchend, but on the ground it hugs the hedgeline to the left and then bears right, going gently downhill to merge with the mapped path at a cartbridge. Climb a headland to reach Churchend Farm by a linked pair of thatched cottages.

The shorter walk turns left here, following a cinder byway to a path junction by an oak tree at an S bend. Maintain direction towards Fir Plantation of Quendon Park. At a T-junction by the trees, turn left on a headland, rejoining the longer route.

The longer walk turns right. to reach a road near Rickling church. Turn left for 400 yards, taking the second footpath on the left. The waymark is only 80 cms high and the eastward mid-field path extends to a white plastic marker tied like a bird scarer in the far hedge. The offset gap gives access to the next path which heads SSE through the crop to reach a grassy headland extending northwards from Brick Kiln Lane. Cross the track and resume the south-eastwards direction, descending to the valley of a small stream. Cross a bridge under power lines on wooden poles. Follow the excellent mid-field path beyond to the woodland around Rickling Green. Turn right on a headland as far as the first dwelling, then enter the woods and select paths which head south-eastwards from the garden fence to reach a transformer on stilts by the cypress hedge of Maples. Go past Spinney Cottage's garage to emerge on the Green opposite the school and the Cricketers Arms Inn. Go left along the road to join the B1383, and left again to pass the covered **fountain**. Opposite the last gate of Rickling House a path leads right under fir trees by a paddock. Take this, and turn left on a path cleared through a thicket passing a cemetery to reach the ornate turret of Quendon church. Go down the church's drive and cross the B1383 to reach a path which rises around the northside of Orchard House's outbuildings. Beyond the paddock rails, join the southward path briefly before turning westwards on a headland down to the brook. Cross a bridge and climb Hanging Hill, to round the corner of trees at the crest and then follow the headland down and up beside Fir Plantation to rejoin the shorter as it reaches the headland from the left.

Pass Tinney Plantation, to the left, continuing along concrete and then a gravel road by Fairwells. Round the north-east corner of the trees and drop to a stream. Now turn right along a byway, following it back to **St Helen's Chapel**.

POINTS OF INTEREST:

Fountain – The horse trough, now flower-filled, and the octagonal fountain were donated in 1887 by Henry Tufnell in memory of Col. Cranmer-Bing of Quendon Hall. They were restored later in memory of G P Beeman of Manor Farm 1922-54.

St Helen's Chapel – The possible widening of the M11 prompted trial diggings by the Chapel which revealed a Christian cemetery suggesting a large Saxon community. The chapel's flint and pebble structure is probably from the early 12th century.

REFRESHMENTS:

The Coach & Horses Inn, Wicken Bonhunt.
The Cricketers Arms, Rickling Green.

Walk 27   **WRITTLE AND WIDFORD**   4m (6$\frac{1}{2}$km)

Maps: OS Sheets Landranger 167; Pathfinder 1122.
In Hylands Park and the Wid valley.
Start: At 680048, Hylands Park Car Park, Writtle.

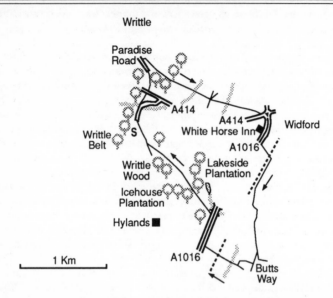

Walk northwards beside the Writtle Belt of trees, leaving **Hylands Park** by underpassing the A414 to join Paradise Road by a gate. On the right-hand side is a recreation ground with a footpath sign pointing between the pond and a pavilion: follow this path, passing another belt of trees surrounding a pond and passing through a corner gap to the arable fields in the valley of the River Wid. The soaring spire of Widford church beckons the path across five more fields: the first three are crossed by re-instated paths through crops. Pass from the first to the second by a culvert bridge over Sandy Brook, from the second to the third by crossing the farm drive east of the cypress hedges, and use a footbridge to cross the Wid. Now follow the fences on the right-hand side as you climb past a plantation and an industrial estate to reach the A414 opposite **Widford St Mary's** church. Bear left to the major road junction and cross, with great care, to reach the Little Chef side of the A1016 dual carriageway.

Turn left to reach a signed footpath, south of Hillside's garden. Follow this mid-field path to the pine trees of Moulsham Thrift Wood. Cross the railway level crossing with great care as it carries very fast inter-city trains.

Turn right along the railway fence until the hawthorn tunnel diverges left, before the river. Beyond the corner of the golf course, the path crosses three feeder streams by culvert, slatted and plank bridges, then heads mid-field for the aerial on the Butts Way AWA pumphouse. Two paths combine to share the compound's drive to reach an unmade road. Pass Highfields, then turn right opposite No. 8, following a fenced path over stiles in the bottom paddock, then going left by the caravan drive fence to reach unmade Bekeswell Lane. Turn right, crossing a bridge over the River Wid. Go under the railway, and cross the carriageways of the A1016, with great care, to reach a bus shelter by Hylands Park boundary wall. Turn right along the verge to reach a permissive stile, on the left, by Lakeside Plantation, into the Park. Enjoy the water features as you walk the parkland grasses to the right of Icehouse Plantation and Hylands House, heading towards Writtle Wood. A path to the right of the trees joins the main drive: go right to return to the car park.

POINTS OF INTEREST:
Hylands Park – The house was built in about 1728 for Sir John Comyns of Writtle. Later Arthur Pryor lived there and he built the two elegant spires seen from the Park today. Chelmsford Borough Council now manage the mansion, arboretum and Park. Much of the Park is a public open space, subject to byelaws. Walking is much enhanced by the permissive outlets and inlets provided originally for the Centenary Circuit in 1988.
Widford St Mary's – The similar spires of Widford St Mary's and Galleywood Church were designed by J P St Aubyn in 1862 and 1873 respectively, having been commissioned by Arthur Pryor (see above). They would have been constructed in full view of the racegoers to Galleywood Common, a popular steeplechase venue from 1795 to 1935. After World War II, the Common, like Hylands Park was bought by Chelmsford Council, and is now a popular open space.

REFRESHMENTS:
The White Horse Inn, Widford
The Little Chef, on the A1016.

LITTLE WARLEY COMMON 4m (6½km)

Maps OS Sheets Landranger 177; Pathfinders 1142 and 1161.

A prospect of the Thames Chase community forest.

Start: At 607906, Little Warley Common Car Park.

Cross Childerditch Lane to the Permissive Footpath sign opposite the car park entrance. Follow the waymarkers down the wooded slope of Childerditch Wood and turn right to walk downstream, with the brook on your left-hand side. The waymarking is consistent, taking the path through meadowland, beside the brook, and under a canopy of trees again by Childerditch Pond. Downside of the dam, take the signed path to the left over a sleeper bridge. Climb beside the right-hand hedge to reach the splendid southern face of **Hatch Farm**. Turn right along a gravelled track, turning left, off it, about 200 yards before the next buildings (Old Shop) are reached to follow a waymarked, field-edge path by The Rookery. The path enters the woodland to contour above an incised brook. Go over a slatted bridge across a baby ravine to reach a junction of paths in the break between Menagerie Plantation and The Rookery woodlands. Go right towards West Horndon, with The Rookery trees on your right.

Next, follow a grassy track by the trees of Pigeon Mount, to the left. Make for a waymarker in a tall cross-hedge: turn right along the hedge to reach a track. Cross the track and the hedgerow to turn south on its western side.

Follow the left-hand hedge around to walk westwards on top of a bank, continuing into the next corner and going over a stile to the scrubland of Jury Hill. The waymarked path now serpentines down the grassy hillock to a footbridge at the bottom. Do not go over the stile: instead, go acutely right, staying with the scrubland boundary to reach a metalled gate into an arable field. Cross NNW to a culvert bridge. Do not cross: instead, walk northwards along the field edge to the next culvert bridge. Cross this and the small field beyond, heading north-westwards to a stile on to a road by Ridgeway. Turn left to a T-junction. Cross and follow the path opposite along a field edge to join a track bridging over a lake's infill stream. Now take the best available cultivation line parallel to the right-hand hedge to reach a road. Turn left, passing an Industrial Estate. Turn right again, as waymarked on the grain store opposite Childerditch Hall. Walk towards the aerial, then leave the concrete to follow a track beyond the barns. Newly planted trees, screening the industrial zone, steer the path to a three-way junction of wires on a pole. Turn right by another new belt of trees, re-entering arable land under wires carried on a series of poles. At the crest of the hill, waymarkers point left as far as the next pole, then right. Follow the hedge northwards, going beyond the end to converge with the wires again by Little Warley and Childerditch Village Hall. Go right along Magpie Lane, passing the Greyhound Inn, as far as White House Farm. Now turn left, uphill, back to the car park.

POINTS OF INTEREST:
Hatch Farm – The farm once belonged to the deer park surrounding Thorndon Hall. The park, landscaped in part by Capability Brown, became farmland this century. Now the area has been acquired by The Woodland Trust, and already the Trust's signs of welcome to visitors are beginning to show.

REFRESHMENTS:
The Greyhound Inn, Little Warley Common.

Walk 29   EAST HANNINGFIELD   4m (6½km)

Maps: OS Sheets Landranger 167; Pathfinder 1122 and 1142.
Good long views, for binocular users.
Start: At 772007, a lay-by on Main Road, East Hanningfield.

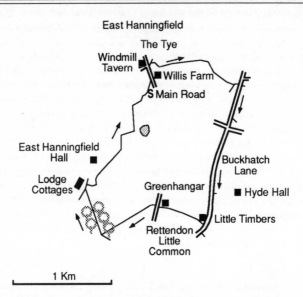

Walk towards **East Hanningfield** and turn right along a tarmac path opposite the Windmill Tavern. Beyond a telephone kiosk the path goes between fences to reach a stile at the rear of the Old Forge. Go over and follow the path beyond to a bridge. Cross and follow a mid-field path to another bridge. Cross the field beyond to some poultry houses. Aim for the white-topped marker post at their southern end. Then turn right along a track and follow it past gas tanks and stables to Leighams Road. Turn right to the crossing of Creephedge Lane. This unclassified road serves as a major thoroughfare between Chelmsford and South Woodham, so cross with care to reach Buckhatch Lane. Pass **Hyde Hall**, to the left, and on the crest by Buckhatch stables and kennels turn right along a bridleway by Little Timbers. Follow the bridleway across Rettendon Little Common, heading for the dwelling displaying four dormer windows between twin gable ends, to reach East Hanningfield Road beside

Greenhanger. Cross to a stile opposite and go over into a paddock to the south of Hillcrest. Cross a stile level with the rear garden fence and follow a path on the northern side of a hedge to a viewing point and path junction.

To the right, downhill, is East Hanningfield Hall and the site of the former church. The path to it appears to be amended slightly from the map's version: follow the hedgeline to an avenue of mature trees and pass down the lane under their branches. Now walk with a hedge on the right to reach Oldchurch Road. Turn right for a few steps to reach a waymarked path, on the right, opposite 2 Lodge Cottages. This path, too, is diverted slightly from its mapped line. Go over a bridged stile in the tight corner under a small oak tree. Follow the right-hand rail of the paddock beyond, as waymarked, through two gates and then turn left beside the northern rail of the inner paddock. Another clever stile and bridge concludes the diversion. Now cross a small field, heading for a stile at the eastern end of the arboretum wall. Go over to reach two paths through the old cemetery: fork right and exit from the eastern side of the wooded graveyard. Now walk mid-field to reach a cartbridge at a junction of ditches about 200 yards short of the tree-lined reservoir banks. Cross and head northwards to a waymarker at the eastern end of a hedge. Turn right towards the reservoir, and resume the northward direction along the field edge. Cross a footbridge over a brook junction and go right, beside a ditch, towards Willis Farm. The path leads to a double plank bridge by a supported pole. Cross and continue through the final field to reach a bridge by the sub-station near the Main Road lay-by near the start.

POINTS OF INTEREST:

East Hanningfield – The village church, of All Saints, has a double location. The churchyard, walked on this route, stood beside a Perpendicular style, brick-built 15th century church, but this was ravaged by fire in December 1883: it was still smouldering as 1884 dawned. By 1885 the present church had been built as a replacement.

Hyde Hall – The Hall's Royal Horticultural Society gardens specialise in outdoor trees, shrubs, roses and bulbs, as well as indoor exotic plants and aquatic features. Openings are organised between Easter and October.

REFRESHMENTS:

The Windmill Tavern, East Hanningfield.

There are also other possibilities in East Hanningfield, and in nearby Rettendon.

Walk 30   STOW MARIES   4m (6$\frac{1}{2}$km)

Maps: OS Sheets Landranger 168; Pathfinder 1123 and 1143.
A walk in drumlinesque countryside.
Start: At 832983, verge parking at Little Hayes Chase, east of
South Woodham Ferrers.

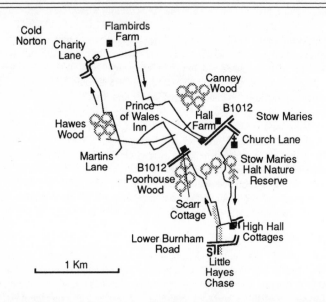

Cross Lower Burnham Road and enter a field by a waymarker. Now walk northwards beside the brook as far as a stiled concrete bridge. Swap sides of the brook and continue upstream. Go over a stile and cross more pasture to reach the wooded embankment of a former railway. Go over the bank, and follow waymarkers to a footbridge and headland beside Poorhouse Wood. Follow the wood edge to reach the B1012 opposite Scarr Cottage. Turn left to the unlimiting speed signs. There, turn right along Path 5. Go over a stile and turn left along Path 3. If this is blocked with barbed wire, follow a diversionary swathe cut NNW through the crop to the parish boundary, from where a change crop aligned left leads towards the radar aerials and almost back to the defined line. Enter a grazing slope and descend south-westwards to reach a stiled bridge. This partially waymarked diversion is not shown on the District Council Office map.

Furthermore, it is offset by another diversion worn south of the obstruction. Things improve as you follow a well-worn, mid-field path to reach Martin's Lane at the south-east corner of Hawes Wood. Turn right, uphill, along a clinkered bridleway, following it to a bend of Charity Lane. Walk ahead (northwards), then bear right along the concrete drive of **Flambird's Farm**.

At a T-junction of drives, go ahead, over the stile by the 'Anglia MFC' sign and head towards the water tower, as far as the fence corner. A horse jump, rather than a stile, gives access to the south side field: follow the fence line, crossing another steeplechase jump and regaining views of the Crouch estuary from a stile in a hedge by the corner pond. Go over and zig-zag with the left-hand hedge. Cross the drive from Hall Farm and go over the stiles controlling a south-eastward, mid-field path to reach the gardens behind the Prince of Wales Inn's car park. The B1012 is reached on the eastern side of the inn: turn left and climb the hill to the Church Lane junction. Turn right, along the lane, passing Smythes Hall and then turning right through the Reg Tavener gates into St Mary's and St Margaret's Churchyard. Walk westwards to reach a step-down stile. Cross this, and three further stiles as you walk through paddocks. A fourth stile leads to a hedgeside squeeze and a fifth stile. Go over to swap sides of the hedge just before entering **Stow Maries Halt Nature Reserve**. Cross the former railway and a double plank footbridge to reach another portion of the sturdily fenced pastures walked earlier. Follow the left-hand fence through two plots to reach High Hall Cottages. Turn right down to a stiled, concrete bridge rejoining the outward route. Retrace your steps back to the start.

POINTS OF INTEREST:
Flambird's Farm – Flambards, now Flambird's Farm has been lived in by a long line of nobles and gentry. Nortuna, now Cold Norton, including Flambards, was ascribed to Ralph Baynard in the Domesday Book. As he had another 24 manors in Essex, he may not have lived here !
Stow Maries Halt Nature Reserve – The Halt was on the West Maldon to South Woodham railway line. The area around the dis-used track is now managed as a Nature Reserve by the Essex Wildlife Trust, its thick belts of scrub controlled to offer habitats for both flora and fauna.

REFRESHMENTS:
The Prince of Wales Inn, Stow Maries.

Walk 31   GREAT CANFIELD   4¼m (6¾km)

Maps: OS Sheets Landranger 167, Pathfinder 1097.
By stockproof hedging and tile clad dwellings.
Start: At 589184, a lay-by near Hayden End, Great Canfield.

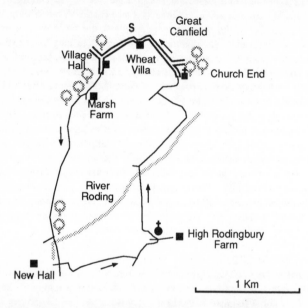

The small lay-by lies between the Polo Centre entrance and Wheat Villa.

Walk westwards towards Helmans Cross and turn left at the junction by Pound House. Pass the Village Hall and continue past the entrance to Marsh Farm. Now leave the buildings on the left to go along a bridleway, forking right by horse chestnut trees. The bridleway is double banked until it clears the marsh, and then becomes a brookside headland to reach a short avenue of trees. Splash through a ford, or use the footbridge, and continue along the hedgeline path until you are between New Hall, right, and High Roding church, left. In the thick stockproof hedge junction is a double plank footbridge, left: cross it and follow the right-hand hedge around two convex corners to reach a cartbridge by an oak tree. Cross, turn left and ascend the slope to High Roding. The path becomes a headland by the reservoirs: continue to a T-junction of tracks. Go straight over, through a gap in the crossing hedgerow and turn left to follow that hedge. Turn with the concave corner to find a bridge left leading to All Saints' Church. From the church gate, follow the track towards the valley, and at its end, go right behind a hawthorn bush to have the fence separating you from any menace by bulls. Turn right by the hedge and follow the fieldside path down to a footbridge over the River Roding.

Over the narrow field back in **Great Canfield**, a junction of field boundaries can be seen, and to the right, at a less obvious junction, a waymarking post is barely discernible against a backdrop of splendid Norfolk reeds. Head for the post and cross a double plank footbridge to walk beside a ditch. Where the ditch bends away left, cross a narrow neck of field to an opposite bend of ditching. Keep the new ditch on your right for a dozen paces to reach a re-instated path crossing mid-field towards the chimneys left of the church spire. Cross a double plank bridge and walk up the slope under wires to reach a track at Canfield Hall. Turn right, keeping the buildings on your right, then swing left by a pond to reach the lych gate at **Church End**. Follow the road past the red mail box to merge with the road to Hayden End. Follow this road back to the start.

POINTS OF INTEREST

Great Canfield – This well spread parish is split into four ends: Bacon End, Hope End, Church End and the lesser referenced Hayden End in the vicinity of Helmans Cross.

Church End – St Mary the Virgin's church, 805 years old in 1995, has graceful proportions enhanced by a seat and a tidy churchyard. The wooden tower is capped by the shingle spire, seen earlier from across the fields. The housing of the settlement has cosy tiled cladding in natural warm colours. The charm of Church End has an allure that makes departure difficult.

REFRESHMENTS

None on the route, but available in nearby High Roding and Hatfield Broad Oak.

Walk 32   **BOXTED**   4$\frac{1}{2}$m (7km)

Maps: OS Sheets Landranger 168: Pathfinder 1052 and 1053.
A walk through orchards, with views in to Suffolk.
Start: At 984314, verge parking at Tye Green, Great Horkesley.

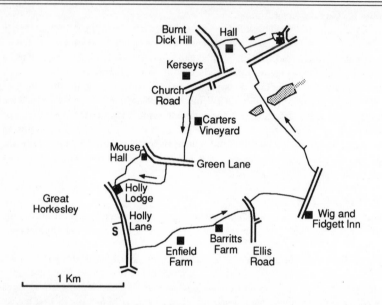

Holly Lane is very pleasant, with cottages sprinkled at random by Tye Green. Walk
south along the lane to reach a signed footpath to the left. Take this, passing Enfield
Farm, to the right, then continuing eastwards through two waymarked hedge gaps to
reach Barritts Farm silo. Just beyond the silo, follow a drive to a road. Turn left on
Ellis Road and as it becomes Workhouse Hill, fork right on to unmade Plantation
Road and follow it to Straight Road. The Wig & Fidgett Inn is to the right, but the
route turns left to reach a red letterbox. Here, take a path to the left, following the left-
hand fence of the grassland and continuing through orchards to reach an old hedge
line along the top edge of a valley.

Paths worn by local dog-walkers give the line down into the valley to a footbridge
across the lake. Climb up the far side between a fence and a tall hedge, and at the top
go right, then left to reach a headland that crosses to Church Road. Turn right and

follow the road to Church Street, on the left. Take this, but after passing the church, turn left on a path to the north of the churchyard, following it to a school. Turn left along School Lane, and then right just beyond the church's western gate. Follow a path along a field edge to Boxted Hall. Turn right by the pampas grass and follow the gravelled track, curving left and contouring through to the road at Burnt Dick Hill. Go left to the T-junction with Church Road. Turn right along the road to reach Kersey's, on the right. Opposite this, go through a gate, and follow the path beyond Carter's Vineyard to Horkesley Green. Turn right along Green Lane as far as the footpath sign left. Follow the left-hand hedge southwards until the mid-field route across to some farm buildings becomes apparent. Turn right on to this path and pass the kindergarten to reach a road at Holly Lodge Bungalow. Turn left to return to the start.

POINTS OF INTEREST:

This walk crosses an area known as Boxted Plain or Horkesley Heath according to the parish. It is an area of Brickearth or Loess soils, similar to those blown in over Tendring Peninsula thousands of years ago. These are interspersed with fluvio-glacial material deposited when the ice sheets of the last Ice Age departed ten thousand years ago. As can be seen, it is now an area of mixed farming with many smallholdings and orchard plots, with the larger fields confined to the vicinity of Burnt Dick Hill. This pattern may reflect the idea of heathland being wasteland as it did not receive priority with the plough. It is only in the present century that cultivation has encroached upon the heaths. Now the loss of heathland flora and fauna is causing alarm and there are attempts being made to save heathers, harebells, sorrels, small copper butterflies, fox moths etc.

REFRESHMENTS:

The Wig & Fidgett Inn, on Boxted's Straight Road, close to the route.

Walk 33   PLESHEY KEEPING   4¹/₂m (7km)

Maps: OS Sheets Landranger 167, Pathfinder 1098.

A fine walk by Walthambury Brook.

Start: At 689139, verge parking by the pump in Bury Lane, Great Waltham.

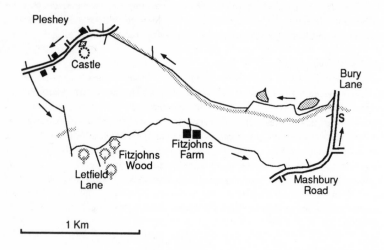

Go north along Bury Lane, then turn left along a track by the reservoir embankment, to the north of the ford. Join a good headland at the north-west corner of the water and follow it WNW through two fields to reach the upper reservoir. Pass to the left of this and follow the headland from the western end of the dam towards a bridge over Walthambury Brook. Do not cross: instead, turn right, upstream, following a path along the edges of two large fields, crossing bridges over all the feeder streams and even one across a minor landslip (although this is best not used because more land has slipped since its placement). Swap to the other bank of the brook where another path comes in to the valley from the north, then cross two more fields to reach the AWA works fencing beyond Pleshey Bridge.

Turn left, up The Street to reach the Leather Bottle Inn by the **Pleshey** village sign and a garden with seats, a good resting place for visitors. Further up The Street, by The White Horse Inn, is Holy Trinity Church and the Community Hall. Walk past these to reach a crossing bridleway beyond the sports field. Turn left along the grassy track to reach a concrete drive to, and across, the valley of Walthambury Brook feeder stream. Now leave the drive by turning left along the softer surface of Letfield Lane, passing a spinney, to the right. Where the lane turns south, go ahead on a track, passing Fitzjohns Wood, to the right. The grassy track, sometimes doubled-hedged, sometimes not, goes eastwards to Fitzjohns Farm. East of the steading, the track surface becomes harder and continues ESE between hedges to reach Mashbury Road. Turn left, passing Little Fellow and forking left along Bury Lane by the red letter box to return to the start.

POINTS OF INTEREST:

Pleshey – The walk passes to the right of Pleshey Castle, today just an earthworks, the castle having decayed or the materials having been removed for construction work elsewhere. The Pump Lane moat bridge is said to be 14th century and is therefore one of the oldest brick bridges in the country. The castle was probably built by the de Mandeville family, originally from Normandy, and was intended as a self-sufficient stronghold against disturbances caused by the Matilda and Stephen struggles. King Richard visited the Duke of Gloucester at the castle in 1389, and asked the Duke to accompany him to London. The Duke never returned to Pleshey, somehow he was murdered in Calais, and the bereaved Duchess stayed there for another ten years. Important routes were guarded by such castles, and it could be that a regular thoroughfare then followed a route similar to the paths of today's Essex Way.

REFRESHMENTS:

The Leather Bottle Inn, Pleshey.
The White Horse Inn, Pleshey.

Walk 34   STAGDEN CROSS   4½m (7km)

Maps: OS Sheets Landranger 167, Pathfinder 1098.

A walk through a fine primrose habitat.

Start: At 638149, Stagden Cross.

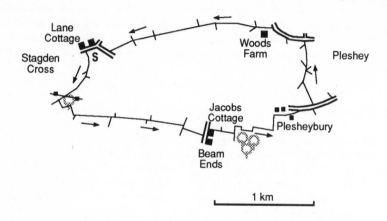

Follow the bridleway southwards from opposite Lane Cottage, eventually bearing south-westwards to reach wooden poles carrying triple cables above the way. Turn left by a new footbridge and cross a field to join a headland running southwards in an arable field. The headland bends left at the next corner and continues over the eastern field edge marked by a reedy ditchbend. The required path runs on the north side of the ditch and there is no bridge: leave the headland to cross the ditch where it is comparatively shallow. Now follow a path eastwards. Overhead wires converge with the hedgeline and then diverge away. Beyond the divergence the path takes a direct line to a shallow valley where there is a plot of shrubland on the right-hand side. Again there is no bridge over the ditch: go right for a few paces to select a crossing point where sturdy young trees provide handholds when negotiating the banks. On the eastern side of the ditch, follow the south side of a hedge to the cartbridge in front of thatched Beam Ends.

Turn left along the road to Jacobs Cottage. Turn right along the north side of its garden cypress hedge. Follow a ditch on the right through two fields to a footbridge. Do not cross: instead, go left, then right along the hedge to a stile. Go over and follow the same hedge until you are level with the eastern end of the thicket. Here another stile allows a swap back to the northern side of the hedge. Continue to reach a footbridge and stile. Cross and turn left along a farm track towards the grey-roofed barns. Turn right, passing the barns, to your left, and a transformer on stilts to reach a stile at the eastern end of Plesheybury lawn. Pass cottages, to the right, go over a stile and converge with the road via the south side of a high thorn hedge sheltering a wide ditch. Walk ahead along the road to a crossing of bridleways by the recreation ground. Turn left, following the bridleway to a cottage at a road junction. Turn left, passing Pleshey Grange, to where the road swings right. There, continue ahead on a byway, pass Woods Farm, to the left. The pleasant track now rises gently to the watershed of the rivers Can and Chelmer. Ignore all turnings to the left and right to reach a road. Turn right to a barn with a cockerel weather vane and start point.

POINTS OF INTEREST:
Primroses are found nationwide, except perhaps near towns where too many plants may be transferred to gardens. In Essex, once a wood and grassland county, the primrose survives mainly in habitats such as those walked on this route: that is in damp and sheltered places. Double hedges covering a ditch discourage agriculture and encourage primroses to blaze their bright yellows in the dappled light filtering through bud-sized leaves.

The Pleshey part of this route is in Chelmsford district where the Borough Council has adorned many public footpath signs with a yellow butterfly symbol. These charming little emblems have won much affection from ramblers, some of whom refer to them as footillary signs.

REFRESHMENTS:
None on the route, but available in nearby Pleshey and High Easter.

Maps: OS Sheets Landranger 167; Pathfinder 1075.
The Flitch Way in the Chelmer Valley.
Start: At 665213, the former station near Little Dunmow.

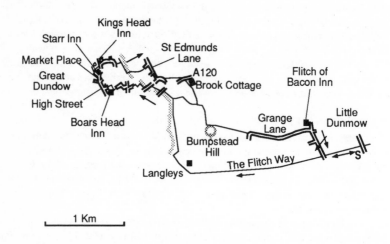

From the old station house, follow the **Flitch Way** westward through a white gate, going along the old railway towards Great Dunmow. The Flitch Way is fractured at an old bridge over the River Chelmer, steps leading down to the riverside. Follow waymarkers to reach a cartbridge.

   The shorter route turns right here, following the hedge as it bears right, then left to reach a path junction by another cartbridge. The longer route rejoins here.

   The longer walk bears left to the old level crossing of the A120. Cross the road, with care, and two fields to reach Braintree Road. Cross and find the north-west parapet corner of the river's bridge. From it a hoggin path follows a fence to Chelmer Drive. Cross Tenterfields at the top of the slope, veering right to enter Venmore Drive. An urban folly beside No. 54 leads past a bowling green to White Street car park. Exit left by the loos to the High Street near the Boar's Head. Turn right to Market Place and descend the slope towards The Downs. Use Star Lane left of the Starr Inn to reach **Doctor's Pond**. North Street forms the eastern edge of the pond: turn left along it to the Kings Head and right into The Maltings. A folly leads left from No. 67 to the riverside. Cross a bridge and maintain direction to climb along a garden fence to the left. Follow Windmill Close and turn right along St Edmund's Lane. Turn left into Stane Street, chasing the sidewalk through to the cul de sac by Ford Farm. When opposite Brook Cottage, cross the A120, with care, to pass to the right of it. Follow the left-hand paddock rail to a gate. Go through and follow a lane to a cartbridge. Cross the field beyond to another cartbridge. Cross, and maintain direction to a yellow arrow on the largest oak tree in the boundary. Turn left by the ditch to rejoin the shorter route at a bridge.

Follow the hedge southwards to a spinney on Bumpstead Hill. Now turn left along a track, swapping sides of the hedgeline about 200 yards beyond the woodland, to join Grange Lane. Walk ahead, along the lane into Little Dunmow to reach a T-junction. **The Flitch of Bacon Inn** is to the left. Turn right down Brook Street. The Priory Church of St Mary's is to the right. Pass the recreation ground to rejoin the Flitch Way at the railway bridge, turn left back to the car park.

POINTS OF INTEREST:

Flitch Way – The Way is an open linear space or country park based upon the former railway line from Braintree to Bishops Stortford, parts of which are open to bridleway traffic and other parts restricted to pedestrians.

Doctor's Pond – The pond was so named because medicinal leeches were once stored there. Tradition has it that an 'unimmergible boat', the forerunner of the lifeboat, designed by Lionel Lukin (1742 – 1834) a London coachbuilder, was first tested as a model on the pond. Lukin, who is buried in Hythe, Kent, designed the *Frances Anne* lifeboat which was launched at Lowestoft in 1807.

The Flitch of Bacon Inn – The inn is named after an ancient ceremonial marriage trial where a flitch of bacon was awarded to the couple in the parish who claimed not to have indulged in quarrels for a year.

REFRESHMENTS:

The Flitch of Bacon, Little Dunmow.
There are also numerous opportunities in Great Dunmow.

Walk 37   LITTLE BADDOW $4\frac{1}{2}$m (7km)

Maps: OS Sheets Landranger 167, Pathfinder 1122.

Grace's Walk and reflective canal waters.

Start: At 762087, verge parking near the Chelmer bridge south of Boreham.

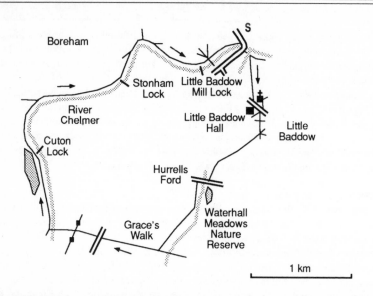

Cross the bridge and turn left on the towpath for 80 yards, going over the blue-railed footbridge at the Sandon Brook confluence, then turning right on a re-instated path up to the square tower of St Mary the Virgin's Church in Little Baddow. Carefully descend the steps that exit directly on to a sidewalk-less road. Turn left, uphill, to the church notice-board, then turn right through the broad orifice of Little Baddow Hall Orchard Farmshop. Go over a stile, then fork left of a hedged pond to get behind the taller store, where diversions are waymarked. Join the nugget-dressed track upside of the stores, and head southwards along it, as the ankle-high arrows direct. Ignore two paths that branch left, but follow one to the right by an established hedge in the orchard. Follow the hedge downhill as arrows show an alternative for Path 13. Go left on the next headland, still as waymarked, towards the tall trees lining the boundary.

Go over a footbridge of concrete joists into a field. Follow Path 13 past a mid-field tree to Hurrells Ford footbridge. Cross, and when south of the brook, cross a road to enter Waterhall Meadows Nature Reserve. Cross the main meadow and pass through the shrubbery at the southern end, where the Sandon Brook meanders near the right-hand hedge. Go over a stile into a field. Follow the left-hand hedge, diverging from the brook, to reach tree-lined **Grace's Walk**. Turn right along the track to Hammonds Road. Cross and follow a mid-field footpath, re-instated to pass a pylon, to reach a cradle bridge in the hedgerow beyond. Cross and follow the path across a smaller field to a footbridge over the **Chelmer and Blackwater Navigation**. On the Chelmsford side of the water, turn right and follow the towpath around by Cuton Lock and downstream a few more feet to reach Stonham Lock. The canal meanders majestically beneath Boreham's settlement to reach another raised footbridge by Baddow Mill. Do not cross: instead, stay on the non-leat side to return to the start.

POINTS OF INTEREST

Grace's Walk – This fine, tree-lined avenue sweeps down from Great Graces across the Sandon Brook towards the River Chelmer. It is reputed to be haunted by a lady who flits through the swirling river mist. Great Graces, at the upper end of the avenue, was the 17th century home of Henry Mildmay. A splendid tomb in Little Baddow Church will tell you more.

Chelmer and Blackwater Navigation – The canal, under construction 200 years ago, is about to celebrate a lusty birthday. Despite the fact that all its commercial traffic has dwindled away, it survives as a linear reservoir, as a source of recreational activity with boating and riparian incomes, and from the sale of timber from the willow trees shading the reflective waters.

REFRESHMENTS

None on the route, but there are plenty of possibilities in Little Baddow and Boreham.

Maps: O S Sheets Landranger 168; Pathfinder 1077.

A walk beside an 'Essexcellent' estuary.

Start : At 065206, the old church, Ford Lane, Alresford.

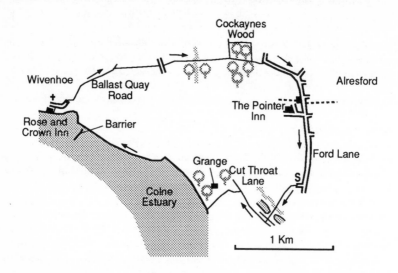

On the Alresford (northern) side of the ruined church a path heads off west, following a bank bottom into the valley of Sixpenny Brook. Cross the brook and climb the isthmus between two pitscapes, industrial remnants now used by anglers. At the top, cross a quarry road cautiously and turn right along the adjacent tarmac of Cut Throat Lane. After about 650 yards, turn left, downhill, towards the Colne estuary on a path that skirts the trees of Alresford Grange. At the bottom the path goes along the old railway embankment which also seems to serve as a seawall.

    Upstream, the path leaves its tunnel of small oaks and broom to chicane on to the seawall proper, which curves, opposite Fingringhoe, towards the **Colne flood barrier**. Development by the barrier has left the alignment of the old shipyard path uncertain, but each new version is well waymarked to ensure you reach the waterside frontage. Pass along The Folly to the Rose and Crown Inn and turn right up Rose Lane,

Wivenhoe. Turn right again to use urban alleyways with houses built from the kerbs. A combination of East and Brook Streets, crossing several junctions, leads to Anglesey Road and a bridge over the railway. Climb from the estuary into Elmstead along this unmade road and then fork right on to a well-used permissive path by Ballast Quay Farm.

Cross Alresford Road and follow a gravelled road eastwards, crossing Sixpenny Brook again. The track continues as an ordinary footpath, crossing a field into **Cockaynes Wood**. The well-worn path leads through the delightful ancient woodland to reach a hedged lane beside an orchard. Follow this to Cockaynes Lane. Turn right, and right again into Station Road. Go over the level crossing to reach a cross-roads by the village sign. Go straight ahead (southwards), following Church Road to Ford Lane and the start.

POINTS OF INTEREST:

Colne Flood Barrier – The barrier is due to be opened in 1994. It has been built despite much local opposition, as a scheme to protect Wivenhoe, Rowhedge and Colchester Hythe from flooding by tidal surges. It was presumably more effective to have a shut-off barrier at this point than to have renewed the seawalls where they are already breached upstream.

The installation of the larger Thames barrier at Woolwich has rendered the entire Essex coastline more vulnerable to flooding. Since the Great Floods of 1953, the combination of global warming and the slight eastward sinking of England has made flood prevention an urgent task for the Rivers' Authority.

Cockaynes Wood – This is an ancient deciduous woodland with manorial boundary banks lacing across its leaf-littered floor. The path followed through the Wood has already been diverted to the northern fringe of the trees to allow felling and subsequent extraction of gravel from deep beneath the roots. Until the extractive process actually starts, the preferred original route is followed permissively.

REFRESHMENTS:
The Pointer, Alresford.
The Rose and Crown, Wivenhoe.
The Black Buoy, Wivenhoe.

Walk 39   BLACKMORE   4¹/₂m (7km)

Maps: OS Sheets Landranger 167; Pathfinder 1122.

In the wooded environs of Mapletree Lane.

Start: At 605022, verge parking in Fingrith Hall Lane, Blackmore.

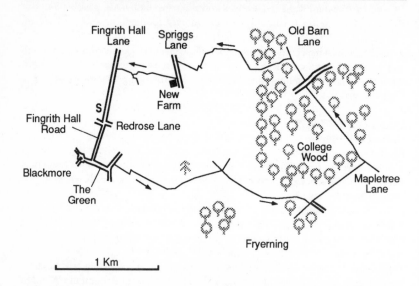

Head south to the Fingrith Hall Lane's junction with Redrose Lane. Cross into Fingrith
Hall Road and follow it to a T-junction in **Blackmore**. Turn left by the display of
pargetting on Swan House and pass by picturesque The Green, complete with stocks,
to cross a bridge over ponds to reach the bus turnaround on Chelmsford Road. Go left
and cross the road under the willow trees to reach a mid-field path that starts by a
green switchbox. Cross the field to an earthen bridge to the right of a pond and follow
the left-hand hedge beyond until it bends away left. There, follow a path that chamfers
a corner to reach a waymarked cartbridge about seven oaks along the hedgerow from
Fryerning Wood. Cross and follow a re-instated path north-eastwards to the cypress
trees by a pond. Now follow waymarks to a lane end. Turn right along an excellent
gravel drive to College Wood. Go over a stiled gate on to a woodland causeway
between old gravel pits. The track passes beside one more small arable field to reach

a junction with Mapletree Lane. Turn left along the bridleway. After about 200 yards the track passes under a canopy of trees that tends to leave the surface damp, and braiding amid the puddles becomes a game to select the best route. Where Mapletree Lane makes an embanked turn to the right, go left, heading deeper into the woodland, following wheelmarks which cross various spring streams searching for the River Wid. Cross Chelmsford Road and use the concrete of Old Barn Lane opposite as far as a waymarker which indicates a left turn. Again braid through the hazel, birch and bracken to locate a planked and handrailed footbridge.

Cross and follow the hedgerow to the right, which diverges from the woodland edge and leads to a double stile. Go over into a large hay field. Stay with the right-hand hedge around by the corner pond to find a stiled footbridge to the next field. Now follow the left-hand headland to Pinmill Cottage on Spriggs Lane. Turn left to reach New Farm, on the right. Turn right by the hydrant and pass through the farmyard to enter a short green lane by a silo. Follow the lane to a pasture, and walk along the left-hand hedge to reach a slatted footbridge. Cross into another field and follow the left-hand hedge to a stiled footbridge alongside another stile and footbridge under the wires. The paths beyond these merge by the pond: follow the right-hand field edge to reach Fingrith Hall Lane. Turn left back to the start.

POINTS OF INTEREST:
Blackmore – St Lawrence's Church, Blackmore has one of the most impressive timber towers in the kingdom, with features similar to classic Nordic stave churches. It is a Norman priory church built in the 12th century for Augustinian canons. Jericho Priory, near the church, sports a polo playing park. When Henry VIII went to Jericho he got no further than the monastery where, it is alleged, he fathered Henry Fitzroy in 1518. The mother, Elizabeth Blount, was later married to Gilbert Talboys, one of Cardinal Wolsey's men.

REFRESHMENTS:
The Leather Bottle Inn, Blackmore.
The Bull Inn, Blackmore.
The Prince Albert Inn, Blackmore.

Walk 40   NAZEING $4^1/_2$m (7km)

Maps: OS Sheets Landranger 167; Pathfinder 1121.

The terrain near Nazeing YHA evokes a buzz of excitement.

Start: At 435055, the Travellers Friend Inn, Epping Green.

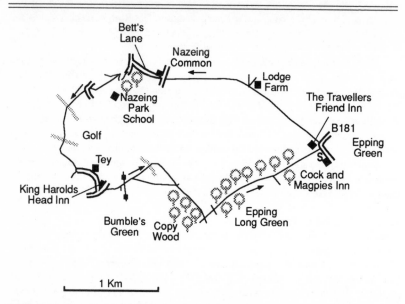

Walk along the east side of the inn car park wall and squeeze between a paddock and a fence to emerge in an arable landscape overlooking Nazeingwood Common. Follow the excellent headland down past a pond and up to Lodge Farm, with a plantation on the left and the farm buildings on the right. Now follow a surfaced track to reach the drive to Nazeing Common. Cross the road to the lily pond and walk along Betts Lane. Go under the trees and turn left at **Hubbards** along the drive towards Nazeing Park School. Before the 1814 building is reached, turn right, before a flat-topped bungalow, and cross the stile behind it. Two paths splay across the grazing: take the left one, diverging slightly from the right-hand hedge to reach a stile in the southern fence. Go over, walk towards the right-hand corner and pass downstream of a pond before climbing to a stile by Rabbit Cottage. Turn left along Back Lane, going around a bend then turning right along a track to a stile on to a golf course. Go over and follow the

78

right-hand hedge to reach a bridge, by a pylon, over Nazeing Brook. Beyond, signs point several ways: follow the track with a hedge on the left heading for the 18th tee. The track takes a short diversion east of a ditch bend to reach a neat brick bridge on to main drive to the clubhouse: cross the drive, and with stream on your right, cross the double plank bridge and stile at the hedge junction. Turn left up the southern side of the hedge and, before a pond is reached, cross to a gate on the right-hand side. Follow the path, doubling back across the fairway to a stile by Belchers Farm and Four Rydes.

Go ahead along Belchers Lane, passing Tays Farm to reach the King Harolds Head Inn at Bumble's Green. Over the road from the inn a signpost indicates The Stort Valley Way: follow this, taking a headland as far as the back garden of Pindars House. Now follow the field edge to the left, ignoring the cradle bridge to the right. Go under the pyloned cables to reach a double plank bridge into the next field. Follow the hedge on the right for 70 yards to reach waymarks offering an alternative to a now-gone bridge. It is a long field edge diversion, crossing a double plank bridge and going around the convex bend of a third field before the ascent to Copy Wood is possible. As the bottom corner of Copy Wood is approached, there is, again, no bridge to join the right of way, so stay eastside of the trees to reach a stile and cross the small pasture beyond to reach a double plank bridge. Cross to join a bridleway at a bend. Turn left, following the bridleway to emerge between the Travellers Friend and the Cock and Magpies.

POINTS OF INTEREST:
Hubbards – All Saints' Church, to the north of Hubbards lies at a latitude of 51 degrees 32 minutes according to its 18th century sundial. Its longitude is close to the Greenwich Meridian. The Norman nave shows post Saxon activity in an area once owned by King Harold, as indicated in several place names.

REFRESHMENTS:
The Travellers Friend, Epping Green.
The Cock & Magpies, Epping Green.
The King Harolds Head Inn, Bumble's Green.

Walk 41   **TIPTREE**   4$^1/_2$m (7km)

Maps: OS Sheets Landranger 168; Pathfinder 1099.

Good views over the former heaths and ramparts around Layer Marney Towers.

Start: At 922173, verge parking near Parkgate Farm, Layer Marney.

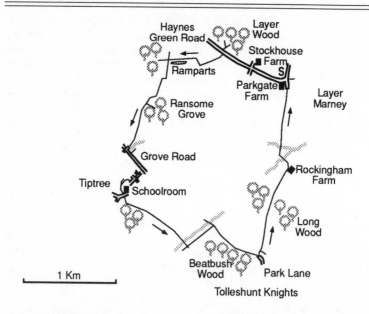

Walk west, passing Stockhouse Farm to reach a cross-roads. Cross into Haynes Green Road and follow it to Layer Wood. Turn left in front of Keepers garage, crossing a footbridge into a large field. Follow the field edge as far as the convex corner to the left, then cross mid-field, northwards, to reach a stile in the matching convex corner. Go over into a pasture with horse jumps and follow the line of the ramparts to reach a bridge carrying the track from Haynes Green Farm. Turn left, southwards, off the anglers' track, on a crop-change alignment to the convex hedge bend. Now follow a field-edge path through two concave corners to reach a path junction by Ransome Grove. Cross the footbridge and head SSW, leaving the woodland, left, at the crest of

80

the slope and following the vestigal hedgeline to Daws Nest. A fence steers the path downhill around two outbuildings to join the drive by a pole. Follow the drive to Grove Road. Turn left, crossing Barbrook and climbing past Rhubarb Hall and the speed limit signs.

Turn right by Whitedawn to use a folly on to Winston Avenue, Tiptree. Turn right again by the sub-station to cross a playing area. Now join Path 25 which leads around by the former **British Schoolrooms** to Chapel Road. Cross, passing Rosedene and approaching Birch Wood. Bend left with the garden hedges and exit from the eastern corner of the wood. Descend to the valley of Layer Brook on a superb headland path, cross a bridge and turn left, downstream, on a field-edge path to reach an unbridged junction of paths at the bottom of Park Lane. Turn right and climb the bridleway past Beatbush Wood, to the right, to join a road by an AWA station. Do not follow the road: instead, go left through the field entrance between the corners of two gardens and follow the field-edge path heading NNE through two fields. Cross a third field to a stile and gate at the edge of Long Wood. Go over and follow a leafy path to a broken stile. Cross the middle of the field beyond to the corner of Rockingham Farm buildings, by the fuel tanks. Turn left along the farm drive, crossing both Layer Brook and Barbrook and then climbing to reach Parkgate Farm.

POINTS OF INTEREST:
British Schoolrooms – The Schoolrooms beside Tiptree United Reformed Church date from 1844. The vicinity of the original room was known as Goodman Green then in the parish of Great Wigborough. The Independent Chapel which fostered it dates from 1750. Tiptree became a civil parish in 1934.

Layer Marney Tower, close to the start of the walk, was built to rival Hampton Court. The first Lord Marney, who was Privy Councillor to Henry VIII, started the project. He died before the building was finished and it has remained an incomplete copy of Hampton Court ever since. It is now a family home open to the public on specific occasions, and includes a rare breeds centre and deer farm.

REFRESHMENTS:
None on the route, but there are several possibilities in Tiptree.

MAYLAND CREEK $4\frac{1}{2}$m (7km)
or 9m ($14\frac{1}{2}$km)
Maps: OS Sheets Landranger 168; Pathfinder 1123.
A coastline declared an environmentally sensitive area in 1993.
Start: At 925021, the lay-by near Newhouse Farm, Steeple.

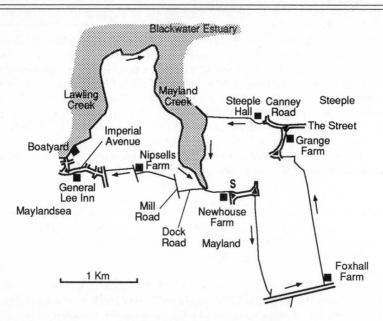

Go eastwards along the road towards Steeple and enter the next lay-by. Turn right along a waymarked path beside the wall of Loftman Farm, continuing along the right-hand hedge and cross a ditch into a field. Follow a re-instated path to a footbridge. Cross and chamfer the corner of the field beyond to a gap in the western hedge. Go through and head southwards to Highlands Farm and the road beyond. Turn left along Foxhall Road, then turn left up a headland on the left side of Foxhall Farm. Cross three fields close to hedges, then the middle of a fourth. At the lower level, follow the right-hand dyke until a field away from a farm, where waymarks point left, away from a new plantation. Join a road by a converted 1877 chapel and turn right to reach The Street in Steeple. Turn left into Canney Road, and where this bends right, walk ahead, passing Steeple Hall Farm pond and a building to the right. Follow the right-hand fence to the seawall of Mayland Creek. Turn left and follow the creek edge to the old dock at its head. Now walk along the eastern side of creek's drain for half a dozen paces to reach a rubble track.

The shorter walk turns left along this track to reach Newhouse Farm. Continue to the road and the start.

The longer walk continues around the head of the creek, then follows a cinder track on the left through a thorn tunnel. This is the former Dock Road: follow it, then turn right along Mill Road to the Sewage Treatment Plant. Turn left, with the fence on your right, and cross a drain on a concrete bridge. Cross the grazing beyond to reach a lane south of Nipsells Farm. Turn right, then bear left around the rear garden fencing of the estate on the left-hand side. The path has a hardened surface in places and urban footways connect left with the estate. Turn left along The Drive for a few strides, then follow Imperial Avenue, passing the General Lee Inn. Bear right at the bus turnabout and cross The Esplanade to reach the waterfront of Lawling Creek. Turn right along the seawall path, going through **Cracknell's boatyard**: the pathway has steps down the slipway and up the other side. The wall walk serpentines around by Harlow's Sailing Clubhouse, becoming an ordinary wall by the arable fields. Stay with the wall: the creek unites with the **Blackwater Estuary** at the same opening as Mayland Creek, that is by Mundon Stone Point, south of Osea Island. Follow the seawall up the next Creek, stiles punctuating the elevated, and sometimes muddy walk, to reach with the eastern end of Dock Road again. Now reverse the route for a few yards and follow the shorter walk back to the start.

POINTS OF INTEREST:

Boatyard – Motor Torpedo Boats and Fairmile Motor launches were built secretly and prolifically at the Maylandsea Boatyard during World War II by Cracknell Bros. These craft were used to hunt and destroy submarines and were influential in raids such as that at St Nazaire. Now the boatyard is dedicated mainly to recreational boating.
Blackwater Estuary – The Song of Maldon in the Anglo-Saxon Chronicle tells of the defeat Earl Bryhtnoth suffered at the hand of the invading Olaf Trygvasson at the Battle of Maldon on 11 August 991. The Vikings used the huge inlet of the Blackwater Estuary to get well inland, camped on Northey Island, visible from this walk, and attacked the Saxons over the causeway.

REFRESHMENTS:
The Sun & Anchor, Steeple.
The General Lee, Maylandsea.

Walk 44   **RIDGEWELL AND BIRDBROOK**   4$\frac{1}{2}$m (7km)

Maps: OS Sheets Landrangers 154 and 155; Pathfinder 1028.

A walk over the Stour to Suffolk and back.

Start: At 737415, Meeting Lane, Ridgewell.

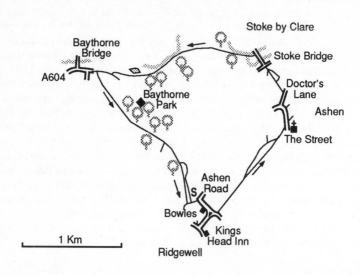

Walk past Bowles Farmshop, **Ridgewell** and across the junction to Tilbury Road. Opposite the first bungalow, right, a waymark is hidden in the cypress hedge: mount the bank and follow a re-instated, mid-field path to the opposite hedge. Now keep this hedge on your right to reach a triple plank bridge in the corner. Cross and follow a re-instated line across the next field towards Ashen church. It should link with a waymark at a third convex corner, but it is slightly off line and carries on to the concave corner before the church. Cross to the smaller field by an oak tree and follow wheel marks to the rear hedging of Bishops Hall. Go along the eastern garden fence to reach The Street, Ashen. Turn left, downhill, passing Street Farm and a moat on the left, then right along Doctor's Lane by Ashley House. Where the wire passes overhead, go over a stile on the left and cross mid-field towards the buildings of Stoke by Clare. Go over a cartbridge and follow the right-hand boundary of the field beyond to reach a

84

T-junction at Stoke Bridge. Walk ahead into Suffolk, and go over the stile at the end of the left-hand meadow. Walk beside the garden fence of No. 65, cross two bridges over weirs and sluices, and continue beside the water until the meadow narrows under willow trees. Go over a stile south of a trough, then cross a footbridge back into Essex. Go through a little wilderness by a small pond to emerge at the corner of a huge arable field.

A good field-edge path follows the lower boundary by an old river course. Where the **river** meanders back to the pathside, do not cross the mesh bridge over the Stour: instead, cross the five plank bridge into the next field and walk beside the river. Ignore another anglers' mesh bridge, then go over stiles into, and out of, a plantation of saplings. Now cross a stile left of a lagoon and walk along a river terrace to a squeeze stile, by a pair of spherical bollards, on to a drive. Go ahead, along the drive, towards Baythorne End. Just before the ornamental gates, turn left through a person-sized gate by the Lodge's hardstanding and head for the gap between a boundary hedge and a fenced plantation. From here, the route to the old barn to the right of the park mansion and trees is better seen. The climb out of the Stour valley continues over the stile beside the barn. Go along the edge of a field and then along a headland in a relieving tree-line re-entrant. Next, follow a mid-field, re-instated path to a triple plank footbridge. Cross into the final field, where a good field-edge path, against the hedge of the orchard, left, is followed to reach Meeting Lane near the northern end of the byway. Turn left to the start.

POINTS OF INTEREST:

Ridgewell – The village is well settled on a ridge, shedding its waters south to the Colne and north to the Stour. There is a well on the ridge, but the name descends from Riddes, an early settler on this lofty site. Ridgewell was more important when traffic on the Haverhill to Hedingham road took two days longer than today's 20 minutes, with the consequential exchange of goods, ideas and trade at the overnight stop.

River – Moorhens may well be seen or heard along this riverside walk. They are similar in size and general colouring to the better known coot. Instead of a white patch above the beak, moorhens have white side flecks. The beaks are red with yellow markings. With hen-like feet their swimming action is jerky and lacks the paddling power usually found in waterfowl.

REFRESHMENTS:
The Kings Head Inn, Ridgewell.
The White Horse Inn, Ridgewell.
The Red Cow, Ashen.

Walk 45　　**Matching Tye Green**　　$4^1/_2$m (7km)

Maps: OS Sheets Landranger 167; Pathfinder 1097.
Is this the Dukedom of Omnium?
Start: At 536112, the pond, Matching Green.

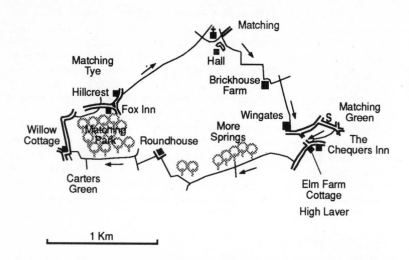

The Green is laced with paths: use them to head southwards towards the Chequers Inn. Go right along the Green's fringe to turn on to a road, signposted 'High Laver', by Elm Farm Cottage. Turn right along the path which begins at the stile opposite 29 Colvers. Cross to a stile by a small pond, serpentine through the grazing beyond and wriggle through the corner railings to reach a bridge into an arable field. Follow the ditch to the right to More Springs woodland corner where a waymarker points to the next corner of the woodland. A woodside path takes you to the final corner, and is followed by a mid-field path, waymarked with white posts, to a stand of trees. Cross a bridge to reach a path fork by the trees. Take the right branch, rounding the spinney and crossing to the convex corner of a high hedge. Follow the hedge NNW to a road by Roundhouse. Turn left and continue ahead along a bridleway after the road bends right. Walk down to a bridge, by a gas marker, and around to the south-east corner of

Matching Park woodland. Follow the dragonfly waymarkers of The Stort Way along the southern edge of the trees to reach Carters Green. Approach the grain store along the drive from the south, bear left and join the road opposite Willow Cottage.

Turn right, following the road around to the north-west corner of the Park. Turn right into a playing field, pass the soccer pitch, the mound and the outdoor gymnasium and bridge to a switchbox by the opposite footpath. Turn right along the road to the Fox Inn, Matching Tye. Fork left behind a bus shelter to Homefield, and turn right along a path opposite Hillcrest. The path is part of The Forest Way, linking Matching Tye with **Matching**. Where it crosses a bridleway, a tarmac private road to Collins Cross, turn right by the pond and cottage (1864) to view the celebrated **Marriage Feast House**. Enter the churchyard, leaving by the roofed noticeboard and taking the path opposite, by the moat. Descend to a stile, go over and follow a mid-field path towards Brickhouse Farm. The initial section is minus the mapped kink en route to the hedge end by a concreted area, the second section has the pronounced kink as mapped. The third phase defers the mapped left turn until the eastern end of a grassy strip is reached by Brickhouse farmstead. Follow waymarkers to join the drive, heading eastwards. Cross a brook and immediately turn right along a field-edge path to the Matching Green sports pitches. Go over a bridge to the south of the western penalty area and follow a fenced path on the Green by Wingates. Ahead is the Green with the pond to the left.

POINTS OF INTEREST:

Matching – Anthony Trollope, as a civil servant, introduced pillar boxes for letter post. As a prolific novelist, his works included the political series of novels sometimes called the Paliser Novels. Plantagenet Paliser, the character central to this series, is depicted as Member of Parliament for Matching, elevated to Duke of Omnium. Fictional names of course, but is there a geographical connection?

Marriage Feast House – For details of this fascinating 15th century building, and for a plethora of facts about St Mary the Virgin church, about trades and customs around The Green, and much else besides, purchase a copy of *A History of Matching* from the church for just 50p.

REFRESHMENTS:
The Chequers Inn, Matching Green.
The Fox Inn, Matching Tye

Walk 46   **THAXTED**   4¹/₂m (7km)

Maps: OS Sheets Landranger 167; Pathfinders 1050, 1051, 1074 and 1075.

The beautiful countryside of the upper Chelmer valley.

Start: At 611311, Margaret Street Car Park, Thaxted.

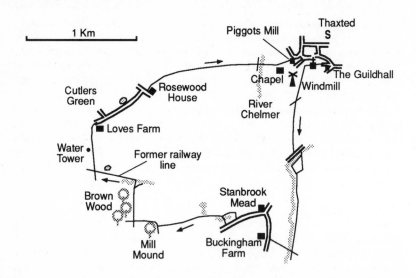

From the car park in **Thaxted,** cross to Margaret Gardens and use Bell Lane to reach Watling Street. Go downhill, cross to the Guildhall and climb Stony Lane to the churchyard. When adjacent to the Bullring, without leaving the precinct of the mighty tower, turn left along the path between the Almshouses and Mill Row. Pass the Windmill picnic site and follow a green, mid-field path southwards with the young river Chelmer a field's width away to the right. Reach the B1051, pass the front of Parkstyle Cottage and cross, with care, to the white-railed footbridge. Cross the incised brook and follow it downstream to its confluence with the Chelmer. The broad grassy headland is a substitute for the mid-field line shown on the map. Continue beside the river, heading downstream for a couple of fields then crossing a cradle bridge under some pole-supported wires. Head for the transformer in silhouette on a pole, between white Morris Cottages and black Buckingham Farm buildings, to reach a road by the Barn Nursery. Turn right, uphill, to a junction. Go left, signposted B1051 Broxted, to reach Path 42, on the right by the crossing wires. There is no signpost, or a bridge over Stanbrook, but the water tower is a beacon. A worn diversion appears at the end of the high hedge on the right of the road where a headland gives access to the northern side of the brook.

Walk beside the brook, around a bend under the wires, to reach a piped section of the stream. Cross westward to the inflow end of the pipe and maintain direction along a shallow gully. At the hedge, continue westwards, with a hedge on the right, through two fields to reach a bridleway by Mill Mound. Continue to a cross-tracks by heaps of soil and spoil together with earth-moving machinery. Turn right, northwards, passing Brown Wood, to the left. The track swings right at the bottom: continue northwards for a few more paces to reach the former Elsenham to Thaxted railway line. Turn left and walk gently uphill towards the water tower, passing a pond before turning right to pass the tower and Loves Farm. The path reaches the Cutlers Green cul-de-sac: walk ahead to the Green. Cross Bolford Street and follow the path opposite, between Rosewood House and a cypress hedge. The magnificent spire of **Thaxted Church** can now be seen across the Chelmer valley. Follow the path mid-field across two fields, then follow a headland down to a brick arch bridge by a cross-paths. Walk ahead, climbing a grassy bank close to the Chapel's cemetery to reach Watling Lane by Piggot's Mill. To the right is The Bullring and Newbiggen Street, with Margaret Street behind the Swan Inn.

POINTS OF INTEREST:
Thaxted – The town's quaint streets attract art as well as commercial craft. From a manorial charter issued in 1205, Thaxted developed a market in the 14th century and became a centre for the cutlery trade which, together with wool, was central to the town's prosperity. The Guildhall dates from 1550 and John Webb's Windmill from 1804. The annual Morris Dance Ring attracts 300 dancers each June.

Thaxted Church – The Church of St John the Baptist, Our Lady and St Lawrence has cathedral proportions. Building began in 1340 and it took seven or eight generations of builders to complete. The 1881 fire which cleared the space for today's Bullring, thankfully missed the church. The spire, pointing high above the clockfaces, dominates the scene for a mile or so in several directions.

REFRESHMENTS:
Many tastes are catered for in Thaxted.

Maps: OS Sheets Landranger 167; Pathfinder 1097.
Range over Wood Green and through Hatfield Forest.
Start: At 536184, verge parking on Wood Row, north of Hatfield
Broad Oak.

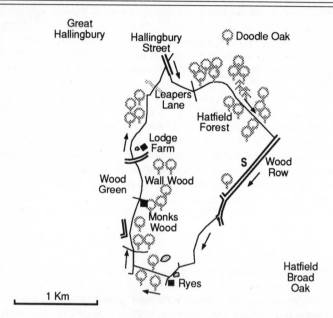

Head south along Wood Row and bear left at the T-junction. Fork right along Ryes
Lane, a private road which is also a public path, to reach a gate under the trees by the
moat and farm buildings. Go through and follow the right-hand track which dips
under a leaf canopy and crosses a stream. Continue mid-field to the tree-lined field
boundary. Go right into Woodside Green by the white gateposts. Woodside Green is
a National Trust open property and offers good walking despite the divots in the turf.
Follow the western edge of Monks Wood northwards and cross a lane to the cottage
by the north-west corner of the woodland. Maintain direction over the next part of the
Green, with Wall Wood well over to the right. Head for the white picketing around
the cattlegrid at Lodge Farm, and when you are by a stand of young trees, about

200 yards before the white fencing is reached, fork left along a worn track towards a waymarker in the hedge to the left of the garage-sized byre. Cross the road and a stile and follow a change-crop alignment northwards, mid-field, to a waymarker to the west of the pond in Lodge Farm's ornamental garden. The path now deflects north-eastwards, but is still mid-field. Go across a lane, and aim for the lime tree with mistletoe at the south-east corner of the woodland.

Go over a cartbridge and bear left to follow the eastern edge of the woodland to the next bridge. Cross and head mid-field to a stile and footbridge in the north-east corner. Cross and walk with a fence on your left to reach Hallingbury Street opposite Street Farm Cottage. Turn right, downhill. The roads bends left to Forest House: go ahead along Leapers Lane to a gate in Hatfield Forest, another National Trust open property. Go through and walk along a broad green firebreak between Lodge Coppice, left, and Emblem Coppice, right. Join a larger track by a couple of box trees. Now leave the white gates of a private property on the left, and head for the stand of conifers in Collin's Coppice. Keep these on your left as a narrower passage is used to reach another broad green track. Beyond the hummocky grasses the narrower path continues south-eastwards from a standing debarked bole of a huge dead tree. Continue through to another vast stretch of grass and follow the left-hand fence to a gate on to Wood Row at the south-east corner of the Forest. Turn right along the road to complete the circuit.

POINTS OF INTEREST:
To the north of the route, Doodle Oak is a marked monument to an old tree said to have grown in the Forest for over 850 years. The vast tree, now replaced by another, is said to have inspired the re-naming of the parish from Hatfield Regis to Hatfield Broad Oak when the forest ceased to have royal patronage. Also just north of the given route through the forest is a lake dating from 1746. Beside it is the Shellhouse Tearoom and Information Centre.

REFRESHMENTS:
Nothing on the route, but available in nearby Takeley, Great Hallingbury and Hatfield Broad Oak.

Walk 48   **LAWFORD**   5m (8km)
Maps: OS Sheets Landranger 168; Pathfinder 1053.
By Judas Gap to Seafield Bay.
Start: At 099326, Stour Sluices, Lawford, on the A137.

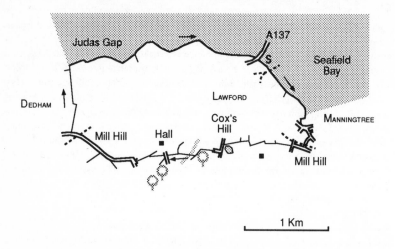

There are several unobstructive parking places, from where grebes, herons and shelducks can be watched feeding.

　　Follow the Essex bank of the Stour, heading for **Manningtree**. Go under the pedestrian arch in the railway embankment, then regain the elevated walkway. Leave the wall by its terminal steps to walk past the Health Centre to reach High Street. Turn left, then bear right up Brook Street from the market place. Go right again to pass under the railway bridge of the Harwich line. Go right up the first Mill Hill on this Walk. Cross Colchester Road to the Lawford open space. Now follow a tarmac path westwards, bending away behind the school sports area to reach a corner stile by the housing. Continue westwards across the field, then dip down below the reservoir dam to join Cox's Hill. Cross, uphill, to reach a lane by the gas station, following it towards

Lawford Church. This dips down and then swings left. Follow the path across a bridge over Wignall Brook then climb to the church.

Select the middle of the three paths emanating from the church. Stiles carry it westwards to merge with Lawford Hall drive. Follow this to Dedham Road. Turn right, with care: there is no sidewalk. Go around a bend to enter the second, and darker, Mill Hill. Dip under the railway viaduct and climb Long Road in Dedham as far as the first dwelling on the right. There, turn northwards, over the stiled gate, and follow the left-hand hedge to another stile. Go over and follow the right-hand fence down to the glorious Stour valley. A double stile gives access to the marshland grazing: follow a path across a field, passing a cattle trough to reach a hand-railed bridge in the northern thorn hedge. Cross this and the field beyond to reach a stiled bridge into a meadow beside Dedham Old River, the name given to a former course of the Stour. Long ago the river was chosen as the county boundary. To the right are the sluices and flood boards associated with Judas Gap, the tidal limit of Stour waters. Stay Essex side, mount the seawall and walk eastwards along it back to the start.

POINTS OF INTEREST:
Lawford Church – St Mary's Church is the home of an annual carol service for cyclists and ramblers. Each Advent the church is packed with pilgrims who have walked or cycled miles to the service. A curious depiction of three dancing figures is found in the nave's 14th-century stained glass panel.
Manningtree – This is one of the smallest parishes, by area in the country, yet it assumes the grandeur of a place the size of Lawford, Mistley and itself all as one. Manningtree's railway junction, secondary school and waterworks, as examples, are all in Lawford. Its church, St Mary's, is shared with Mistley and is a replacement for St Michael and All Angels, Manningtree, which was demolished for safety reasons after World War II. Matthew Hopkins, the 17th-century Witchfinder General, scourge of 200 witches, is associated with Manningtree.

REFRESHMENTS:
The Skinners Arms, Manningtree.
The Swan Inn, Manningtree.
Manningtree Station buffet also enjoys a good local reputation.

Walk 49   DEDHAM   5m (8km)

Maps: O S Sheets Landranger 168; Pathfinder 1053.
A walk through Constable Country.
Start: At 058333, Mill Lane car park, Dedham.

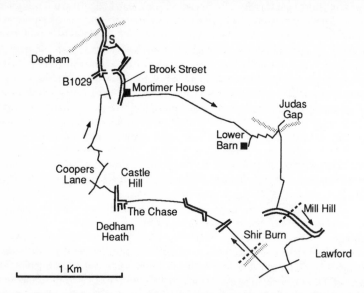

Go over the footbridge to the east to the Rare Breeds Centre. Do not enter the Centre: instead, turn right along a waymarked path through the grounds of Dedham Hall, passing a pond to reach the drive. Follow the drive to Brook Street and continue along this to Mortimer House. Just beyond, turn left on a path by a sub-station, following it across a field to a stile. Go over and cross the field beyond to merge with Chilver Warren fence. Use a headland until the re-instated path leads to a stile to the north of Lower Barn Farm. Go eastwards along a concrete road with squeeze stiles beside the gates to reach a marshland grazing area. Cross this by the causeway to reach a stiled bridge near Judas Gap. Do not cross but turn right (south) to cross the same grassy plot to a stile and handrailed bridge in the southern thorn hedge. Continue south across several fields linked by stiles to reach a road near a dwelling. Turn left, with care, going under a railway bridge and climb the wooded cutting of Lawford's Mill Hill. At the top, turn right along a bridleway, following it to a gate by a dwelling. Go through and follow a drive through another gateway, after which it swings through a wooded hollow. Beyond this, turn right, as waymarked, down a slope, through trees and over causeways to reach a bridge over Shir Burn and some old watercress beds.

Cross the railway, with great care, then continue over a series of stiles and paddocks to reach Long Road. Cross into a field and head north-west to reach a stile on to East Road. Turn right, go around a left-hand bend, but at the next (right-hand) bend, continue ahead on a path that crosses further stiles, paddocks and pastures to reach a lane 'The Chase' in Dedham Heath, with the Anchor Inn around the corner to the left. Turn right (north) along Crown Hill for about 200 yards to reach a waymarked path to the left. Take this, crossing the grazing to dip to a stile under trees by the back garden of Orchard House. Go up the garden path, turning at the front on to the drive out to Hunters Moon. Turn right along Coopers Lane and take the drive, downhill left, by the timbered house to reach a stile. Go over and follow a path to the north of stables. Cross a paddock and a bridge over Black Brook, continuing on a path that joins another at a stile. Go over and cross two fields, heading towards the church. Go right, then left behind the cricket pavilion and pass the Duchy Barn Countryside Centre to reach Royal Square, **Dedham**. Straight ahead is Mill Lane and the car park.

POINTS OF INTEREST:
Dedham – Sir Alfred Munnings is associated with Dedham. President of the Royal Academy for five years after World War II, his studio was at Castle House. Details of opening times are available at the Duchy Barn Centre. Munnings is best known perhaps for his paintings of horses. John Constable lends his name to the entire surrounding countryside. John was born in 1776 at East Bergholt on the Suffolk side of the river, and attended school in Dedham. Several of his celebrated paintings are of the Dedham Vale.

REFRESHMENTS:
The Anchor, Dedham.
The Sun, Dedham.
The Essex Rose Tearooms, Dedham.

Walk 50　　　　STOURDALE　　　　5m (8km)

Maps: OS Sheets Landranger 168; Pathfinder 1053.

And the Stour goes on for ever.

Start: At 043333, a lay-by off the A12 at Gun Hill.

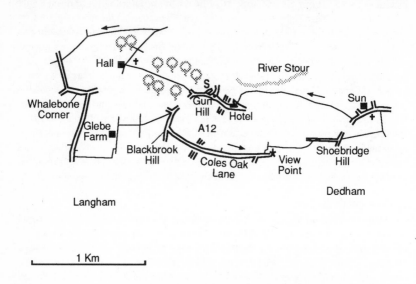

Walk up Gun Hill to the lodge cottage. Turn on to the drive and follow it to Langham church. There, turn right, downhill, on a track towards the River Stour. Turn left at the first hedgerow and walk along the northern side of a spinney to reach a stile. Cross the field beyond to another stile. Go over and turn left up the track to West Lodge. Follow the tarmac up to Dedham Road, turning left by Whalebone Corner. Now turn right on to Rectory Road. After about 650 yards there is a staggered crossing of footpaths: turn left along a path diverted to the southern edge of a field to reach Glebe Farm's drive. Turn left, passing the farm and then turning right along a headland to a parallel drive which heads north-east to Blackbrook Hill. Double back right along the road, then turn left along Coles Oak Lane, over the A12. Now take the second footpath on the left. Fork right when you are behind the dwellings near the old Rectory Farm.

Follow the path through gates and over stiles, then down through a spinney to reach Stratford Road.

Turn right along the road to a T-junction. Cross Shoebridge Hill to the path opposite, following it to the cricket field by **Dedham Church**. Join the path from **Southfields** behind the pavilion, following it past the Duchy Barn conveniences to reach High Street. Cross left to **Sherman House** and the Sun Inn, then turn right opposite Hewitt Hall to approach the National Trust's Bridge Farm. The westward track from the farm swaps sides of a hedge twice before passing a pantiled byre and joining the River Stour. Soon, the path winds around a left-hand garden boundary and rises to the former Dedham Vale Hotel. Go left and round the road junction to pass to the south of the Hotel. Now bridge the A12 to return to the start.

POINTS OF INTEREST:

Dedham Church – Should you be in Dedham for Tuesday breakfast you may hear the church bell ring. This custom dates from 1578 when the Church Lectureship was founded. It meant the vicar had to preach to traders before they could open the weekly market. Both the market and the lectureship have lapsed, but the bell dongs on. A lapsed market suggests a prosperous past, and this is true of Dedham. Wool and woollen products were the foundation of its riches. The large church, with its echoes of Ely Cathedral, is a symbol of that prosperity. People from Dedham, USA contribute to the upkeep of the church as a memorial to their Dedham ancestors who sailed or followed the Mayflower.

Southfields – This is the former Master Weaver's House of the Bay & Say trade. It was built in the 15th century for Robert Cranfer, a clothier who distributed wool for spinning to local cottagers.

Sherman House – This is named after the same family as the Civil War hero and the Sherman tank.

REFRESHMENTS:
The Sun Inn, Dedham.
The Anchor, Dedham.
The Essex Rose Tearooms, Dedham.

Walk 51   HORKESLEY HEATH   5m (8km)

Maps: OS Sheets Landranger 168; Pathfinders 1052 and 1077.

A walk in the rural fringe of Britain's oldest recorded town.

Start: At 984314, verge parking at Tye Green, Great Horkesley.

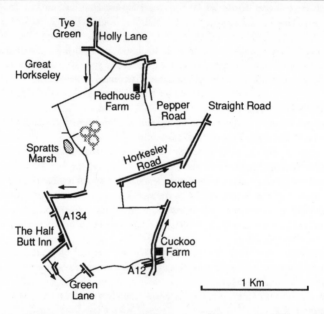

Holly Lane is very pleasant with cottages sprinkled at random by Tye Green: head southwards along it to a T-junction. Turn right for a few paces, then go left along a concrete drive. The drive bends right on Broad Lane. Take next left and follow Lincoln Lane where the pleasant area of open water at Spratts Marsh can be seen. Follow the drive to its end. Go over a stile and follow the path beyond to Ivy Lodge Road. Turn right to reach a T-junction with the A134. Turn left along the road's sidewalk to the Half Butt Inn. Turn right into Brick Kiln Lane. Follow this to 'Tara', and turn left there on to a path to Blackbrook Road. Go ahead along the road following the waymarked path at its end along the edge of a **spinney**. Soon, the path reaches a T-junction with Green Lane. Turn left and follow this to The Causeway. Cross to Terrace Hall and climb the short America Hill to a stile into a market garden area. Path 40 is rarely usable here, so it is easier to follow the right edge around to the parish boundary by the A12 fencing.

Follow the fencing to Cuckoo Farm bridge. Go over a stile and up steps to Boxted Road. Cross to **Cuckoo Farm**, then turn left along the verge, which is narrowest where it is most necessary in the shallow bottom of a blind bend. Turn left into Accommodation Road, passing smallholdings and steadings spaced around its northward bend to reach Horkesley Road. Turn right, then left along Straight Road, following it as far as Langham Lane. Turn left along unmade Peppers Road, extending off the end of the lane on to a crop-change alignment which carries the path just beyond a pole supporting overhead wires. When you are aligned with the convex hedge corner south of Redhouse Farm, turn right across another change-crop alignment to reach the hedge corner. One field further on, the path along the field edge becomes a double hedged track leading to the road by Redhouse Farm. Go northwards along the road, then left on to Queenshead Road, rounding Harrow Corner. Now turn right into Holly Lane to return to Tye Green.

POINTS OF INTEREST:
Spinney – The OS maps show plenty of green for woodland in this area, but alas not much of it remains: Horkesley Plantation is now but a fringe of trees compared to the extent given on the map. Agricultural subsidies for further cereal production have increased clearances in the last 40 years. The deciduous canopies of Harrow Corner and Green Lane spinneys become all the more delightful for the rarity of the habitats they provide.

Cuckoo Farm – This is a working farm with a herd of pigs as part of the enterprise. Some of the buildings, redundant for modern farming practices, have been converted into workshop units suitable for arts and crafts. Newly painted toys may be seen through open craftroom doorways. Opposite, there is a farm shop.

REFRESHMENTS:
The Half Butt Inn, on the route.

Walk 52   WEST BERGHOLT   5m (8km)

Maps: OS Sheets Landranger 168, Pathfinder 1077.
A walk around Pitchbury Ramparts.
Start: At 954281, West Bergholt Church.

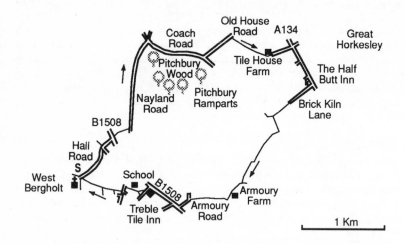

Walk up Hall Road and cross the B1508 road to a stile. Go over and follow the right-hand hedge through two fields to reach a stile on to Nayland Road. Turn left to reach a crossroads. Turn right along Coach Road, passing **Pitchbury Wood**, to the right. Turn left along Old House Road for about 400 yards, then take a signed footpath to the right. Go through an orchard, noting the high, narrow hedges which punctuate the fruit trees. Their job is to control air movement. Follow the path ESE to Tile House Farm. Pass the working area carefully and follow the farm drive to the A134. Turn right along the sidewalk, passing Coach Road and Keelers Way, to the right, to reach the Half Butt Inn. Just beyond, turn right along Brick Kiln Lane. The lane becomes an orchard track bending right when beyond some buildings.

   A grassy headland now dips down the hill to the left: use this as a substitute for the cross-orchard path. Turn right at the bottom and when you are near the corner, swap sides of a ditch at a culvert bridge. Now follow the well-marked mid-field path. Turn right at a hedgerow and climb to Armoury Farm. Pass the farmhouse and turn right along an unmade road (**Armoury Road**), following it to the B1508. Turn right along the sidewalk to the Treble Tile Inn. Just beyond, turn left along School Lane. Soon, go right on a path by the school to reach Lexden Road by the scout hut. Cross to a path that runs along the northern side of Firmins Court and continues mid-field to a fence corner. Now walk beside the fence to West Bergholt Hall and the church.

POINTS OF INTEREST:

Pitchbury Wood – Pitchbury Ramparts, at the southern edge of the Wood, are an oval hill fort, thought to have been associated with the western perimeter earthworks of Camulodunum. Some dating work there indicates occupation during 6th – 4th century BC.

Armoury Road – The block of buildings south of Armoury Road is the site of Daniels Brewery, taken over by a larger company after World War II. The meadowland surrounding the brewery was once graced by grazing dray horses, a magnificent sight.

REFRESHMENTS:

The Treble Tile Inn, on the route.
The Half Butt Inn, on the route.
The White Hart, West Bergholt.
The Queens Head, West Bergholt.

Walk 53 **FORDHAM** 5m (8km)

Maps: OS Sheets Landranger 168, Pathfinder 1077.

Contouring the Colne river valley.

Start: 929271, the anglers' car park at Fordham Bridge.

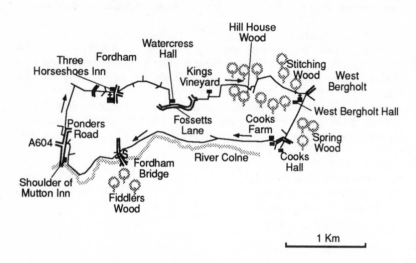

The first dwellings on the Fordham side of the river have public footpaths by their garden fences. Walk north from the bridge, then go left, along the northern side of Mill House and follow a path to the riverside. A good riverside walk ensues, though the river does move away at one stage, to the garden of the Shoulder of Mutton Inn. The path now heads north, away from the river, going behind the gardens to reach Ponders Road. Turn right, but at a sharp right bend, go up steps cut in the bank on the left to reach a field. Follow a mid-field path, not always visible, to reach a headland. Now turn right aiming for Fordham church. Cross a road, uphill, to a notice pleading for careful driving and go through a gap in the nearby thick hedge, an opening for Path 28. Follow this across a field, then north of a paddock to reach a kissing gate into the churchyard. Leave through another kissing gate. Opposite the Three Horseshoes Inn follow Path 21 diagonally across the field to a hedge corner, then along a hedgerow to the right going through three fields to reach a second stile. Go over and walk with a hedge on the left, heading southwards to reach Fossetts Lane by Watercress Hall. Go left, following the road around to the entrance to Kings Vineyard. Follow the drive, approaching the farmhouse and then turn right by an electricity box near a gate. Follow a tree-lined avenue east, then north, and then a field edge path which dips to a footbridge and enters **Hill House Wood** beyond.

Climb the valley side and fork left at two path junctions to emerge on a headland on the northern side of the wood. Follow the headland, which bends right to become a track to **West Bergholt Church**. Turn right and follow waymarks back down to the Colne Valley, passing a transformer on stilts and forking right to reach Cooks Hall Farm. Go right by the pond, pass a silo and head westwards along an unmade road. Dip down to pass a red-brick byre. Go over a bridge and continue to a path fork. The wheelmarks go up right to Chancers, and the single foot-track heads for the south-west corner gate nearer the river: use the riverside option. Follow the hedge on the right to a stile. Go over and follow the riverside to a footbridge. Go over this and another bridge to reach the top of a bank. The river now bears away: follow the path to steps down to a road. Turn left, with care, back to the bridge.

POINTS OF INTEREST:
Hill House Wood – Also known as Bluebell Wood, it has a fine annual display of anemones in April. The Wood was subject to a nail-biting tug of war in 1993 when the parish attempted to raise sufficient money to buy it before it passed to a rival bidder on Boxing Day. Thanks to an anonymous Christmas subscriber, the villagers won, and now manage the wood for the benefit of West Bergholt.
West Bergholt Church – St Mary's is to the west of the settlement, where a replacement church has been built. The disused church has parts dating back to 14th century. West Bergholt Hall next door invariably attracts amused interest, because its Georgian type lines have an urban appearance, and the looker seeks in vain for its neighbours.

REFRESHMENTS:
The Shoulder of Mutton Inn, on the route.
TheThree Horseshoes Inn, on the route.
The Vulcan Inn, Fordham.

Maps: OS Sheets Landranger 167, Pathfinder 1098.
An ideal stroll at the ebb of day.
Start: At 780187, a lay-by on The Street, White Notley.

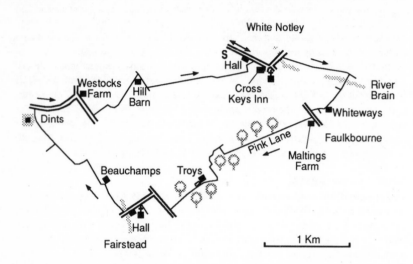

Walk towards White Notley, passing the Cross Keys Inn, then bearing left to cross the river. Turn right along a concrete road by the works compound. At its end, go over a stile and follow the field edge path beyond. Soon a footbridge, on the right, offers a return to the western bank. Take it, climbing out of the little **valley** to have a hedge, then a paddock on your right-hand side before you join the drive of Whiteways. Follow the drive to a road and turn left, towards Witham, as far as Maltings Farm. Turn right along a concrete drive, then follow gravel-surfaced Pink Lane up to the watershed. The lane bends right and then left to become double hedged. It then threads through delightful habitats and eventually becomes the drive of Troys: continue along it to reach the **Terling** road.

Turn right along the road to a T-junction by Fairstead Church. Turn left, passing the church. Go downhill, and at the bottom turn right by a pond to follow yet another concrete track. Go past Beauchamps, continuing past woodland and Dines moat to reach Ranks Green Road. Turn right, then right again to pass Westocks Farm. Now look for the signed bridleway on the left. A headland follows the left-hand hedge across three fields as it rises to the watershed by Hill Farm barn. Turn right along another concrete track as far as the overhead power cables. There, go left on a headland beside the left-hand hedge down to the trees behind the Cross Keys Inn. Swing left by the outbuildings, and right before Hall Farm to reach the road opposite the village hall. Turn left to return to the start.

POINTS OF INTEREST:

Valley – John Ray, 1627-1705, is associated with Black Notley, his birthplace and last resting place, but he probably knew much of the Brain valley through White Notley and Falkbourne too. In his 'Historia Plantarum' of 1648 he lists 20,000 species in great detail. His work set the standard used world-wide today by followers of the 'father of natural history'.

Terling Marthus – Over100 years ago, Edward Strutt took over his brother's estate in Terling at a difficult time for farming. Arable dairy farming, as it was then called, meant growing food for the prime enterprise, which was building dairy herds. Today at Hatfield Peverel is the headquarters of the vast Lord Rayleigh's dairy operation which developed from earlier prudent investment. Any black and white Friesian cattle seen on today's walk could well be related to Terling Marthus, a British Friesian bull of world fame sixty years ago.

REFRESHMENTS.:
The Cross Keys Inn, White Notley.

Walk 55 **TERLING** 5m (8km)

Maps: OS Sheets Landranger 167, Pathfinder 1098.

A walk around Terling Windmill.

Start: At 767168, Hall Road, Fairstead.

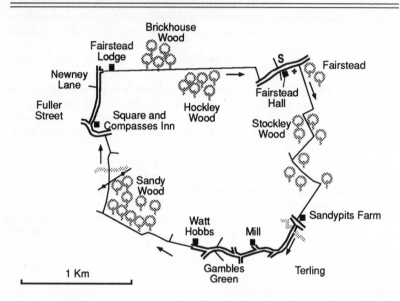

Take the footpath on the east side of the church, going through the churchyard extension. Go over footbridges and a complex of stiles in the shallow valley south of the church and then up a good mid-field path. Turn right at the top and go part way along the northern edge of the woodland to where a plank bridge gives access to a splendid path through Stockley Wood. From the southern edge of the trees, a mid-field path crosses to the hedgerow: turn right beside a ditch and go south of it to find a path heading southwards. Walk with a hedge on your left and then turn right along a track by Sandypits Farm to reach a road on the outskirts of **Terling**. Cross to the road opposite, descending to the footbridge beside Terling ford. Cross and climb up Norman Hill, forking right to pass the smock windmill's lane whilst on Hull Lane. The windmill was the last county mill in commercial operation until a Mr Bonner was crushed there in 1950.

Fork right again on to Waltham Road. Ignore Oakfield Lane, and fork right by the pond into the next cul-de-sac. Pass to the south of Watt Hobb's Farm and continue westwards on a track. Go over a stile and cross a field to the south-east corner of Sandy Wood. Pass the southern and western sides of the wood, then drop under the power cables to reach a stile. Go over this and a footbridge over the River Ter. Go around the spinney corner to get on the right-hand side of a northward-running ditch, following it to Fuller Street. Turn left, passing Rose Cottage, then turn right to the Square and Compasses Inn. Continue up Newney Lane, passing Ashwells Farm and Herons, then turn right along the drive to Fairstead Lodge. Go through the farmyard, with caution, and walk along the southern side of the garden hedge. Continue eastwards to reach a bridge at the south-west corner of Brickhouse Wood. Walk with the woodland on your left, go under the power cables and continue with Hockley Wood on your right. A path now follows the left-hand hedge down and around to the right to join Fairstead Hall Road. Turn left, where a charming scene of the Hall and church heralds a reunion with the starting place.

POINTS OF INTEREST:

Terling – The village is sometimes pronounced to rhyme with Starling. Terling Place is the stately home of Lord Rayleigh: it has also been called a seat of ideas. The current Place is by John Johnson in 1773 and it succeeded one frequently visited by Henry VIII on his excursions to Harwich and East Anglia. The third Lord Rayleigh, John Strutt, was a Nobel Prize winner, the discoverer of argon, Professor of Experimental Physics at Cambridge University and Chancellor of the same university.

Mystery surrounds the charity trust which benefits Terling's inhabitants each Christmas. Henry Smith, a rich London merchant is said to have visited Terling disguised as a vagabond between 1548 and 1627, a time when vagrants were promptly ushered on their way. Smith received good treatment, and left a trust fund for the parish, enough to purchase White House Farm in Tolleshunt D'Arcy. Income has provided for gifts of food and clothing for over three hundred years.

REFRESHMENTS:
The Square & Compasses, Fairstead.
The Rayleigh Arms, Terling.

Walk 56   **GREAT WALTHAM**   5m (8km)

Maps: OS Sheets Landranger 167, Pathfinder 1098.

Georgian taste in the Chelmer valley.

Start: At 705150, verge parking in Hyde Lane, Great Waltham.

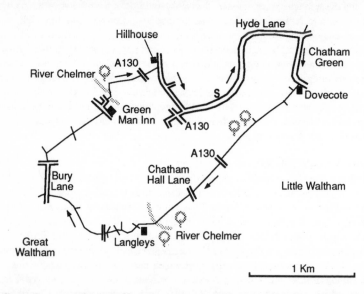

Walk north-eastwards along Hyde Lane, passing The Hyde and Hyde Hall to reach
Liberty Hall. There, turn right towards Chatham Green. Follow the lane past cottage
gardens to the bend by the former Windmill Inn. Now turn right along a green lane by
a dovecote. About 100 yards south-west, the lane opens to an arable landscape
overlooking the Chelmer valley: a green headland follows the right-hand boundary
beyond the bridges by Chathamhall Springwood to the A130. Cross, with care, and
maintain direction to reach a stile on to Chatham Hall Lane. Cross this, and follow the
pleasant green lane opposite to complete the descent into the Chelmer valley. Go
through a kissing gate and follow metal railings to the join a drive where it bridges the
river in the delectable **Langleys** estate. Follow the drive around and over a brick bridge
by the leat's weir, and then around a dwelling, to the right, to pass a pets' graveyard.
Now follow the fenced drive away from the grand mansion. Two paths cross from the

tree belt, to the right, to the twin drive, to the left: cross grazing to the exit stile of the second of these paths, and head for the western red cedar tree north of Great Waltham Church to exit the estate by cottage No. 2. On the western side of the road is a stile by a bus stop: go over and follow the path beyond along the right-hand hedge to reach Bury Lane by a ford and reservoir. Turn right and walk to a T-junction.

Cross into unmade Dunmow Lane, but after four strides, at a transformer on stilts, go right along a path, crossing a field aiming at a white-topped post at the convex hedgebend. From the post, continue with a hedge on your right to a cross-paths in the concave corner. Maintain direction through a gap and cross a field towards the double white gables of the **Green Man Inn**. Go over a stile and cross to another on to a road almost opposite the inn. Turn left, away from the inn, to reach a triangular junction opposite Fitzandrew Cottages. Turn right, but as the lane swings left, go down and cross a stiled concrete bridge over the Chelmer. In the field beyond, take the northern diagonal path to a gate by a weir. Stay by the lesser, right-hand, course of the river as far as a double-stiled bridge. Cross to a grassy causeway across a field. Now follow the left-hand hedge through two small fields to reach the A130. Cross, with care, and climb the headland opposite, passing the cypress screen around the Hill House pool and court to reach a road. Turn right to the foot of the A130 embankment and bear left along Hyde Lane back to the start.

POINTS OF INTEREST:

Langleys – This handsome mansion has been extended and modified with great care and taste since 1711 when it was sold by the Everard family succession to the Tufnell family. The grandeur of such continuity seems to include timelessness at first, but the passing walker can soon appraise the remorseless energy needed to sustain the estate in step with time.

Green Man Inn – The Inn, in Howe Street, is said by many a rambler to be the oldest still serving beer in Essex. Rambling groups in this area have mandatory visits to the Green Man.

REFRESHMENTS:
The Green Man Inn, on the route.
The Great Waltham Inn, Great Waltham.
The Beehive, Great Waltham.
The Six Bells. Great Waltham.

Walk 57   MARGARET RODING   5m (8km)

Maps: OS Sheets Landranger 167; Pathfinder 1098 and 1122.
Beautifully hedged bridleways, but best when dry!
Start: At 621109, Salts Green lay-by on A1060

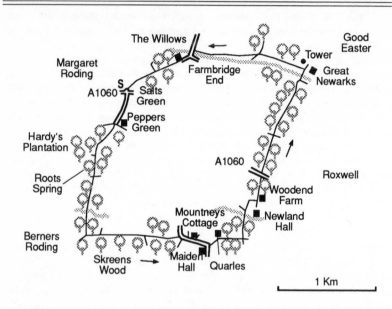

Cross the A1060, with care, to follow a lane signed to Peppers Green only. The tarmac ends at Peppers Cottage: select path 17, a hedged bridle-cum-byway. Go past the trees of Hardy's Plantation and Roots Spring, with their attendant path junctions, and cross Newland Brook to reach a path T-junction. Turn left to bypass **Skreens Wood** on a headland with hedge on its right-hand side. Later the path gains a left-hand hedge when it merges with a vehicular track. Continue eastwards over a staggered cross-paths as a lane is joined, maintaining direction until the Maiden Hall bend is reached. Here, fork left on a bridleway, passing to the right of Quarles and continuing to the Newland Spring cross-paths. Turn left.

Re-cross Newland Brook by the willow trees, then, by Newland barn, cross a concrete drive and follow the bridleway uphill, as indicated by the Chelmsford Council sign bearing the yellow 'footillary' emblem. The path bends right by a paddock to join a lime tree lined lane at Woodend Farm. Go left to the A1060. Cross, again with care, to a continuation bridleway, following it to the reservoirs in the Can valley, by Great Newarks. Here, two tracks unite with the northern end of the bridleway to share a diagonal path across the grazing to the Can bridge by the steading's garden. Approach a tower with a pond on your left, then turn left, between the pond and a transformer on a pole, to walk beside further water.

A tumbled gate marks the entry to a field: hug the right-hand hedge around the curved boundary to a stile over the electric fencing. Cross the field beyond to a stile in the hedge where there is a footbridge over Chalybeate Brook. Ten paces right is a Y-junction of tracks: select the western one, walking parallel to the river, following the right-hand hedge through two fields to a reach a stile at Farmbridge End. Turn left, crossing the Can, then fork right along a byway. The tarmac gives way to grass by The Willows as the byway climbs the valley, as a headland after the path junction, back to Salts Green.

POINTS OF INTEREST:
Skreens Wood – Among the wild deer herding through Essex are muntjacs, or barking deer. They are recent arrivals, being descended from Woburn escapees, having originally been brought from Asia. They are about 18 inches (45–50 cms) tall at the shoulder and sport a reddish coat, lighter when in summer shade and appearing darker with the winter fur. They browse rather than graze, and can be found wherever brambles, ivy and young shrub growths are available. Small woodlands like Skreens are ideal cover for them. When alarmed their short tail is held erect to reveal a white scut as the animal bounds for cover.

REFRESHMENTS:
None on the route, but available in nearby Roxwell, Good Easter and Willingale.

Walk 58   **HIGH ONGAR**   5m (8km)

Maps: OS Sheets Landranger 167, Pathfinder 1121.
In the valley of the River Roding.
Start: At 561041, the old Chelmsford Road Bridge.

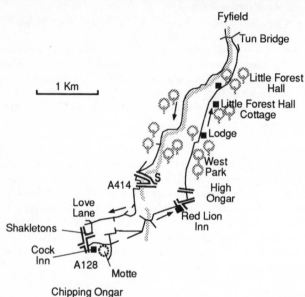

The A414 road has been upgraded and a new bridge over the Roding between Chipping Ongar and High Ongar has left a convenient parking place by the old bridge on Chelmsford Road.

Approach Chipping Ongar via the stile on the A414 side of the road. Pass under the bridge beside the Roding and use the waymarked path to the black gates by the A414. Turn left on a headland and swing right with it through another metal gate, ignoring the mapped hypotenuse path. Approach the housing and pass through it and a playing field to reach the Parish Council Office at the top of Love Lane. Go left beside the recreation ground, then turn right down Shakletons to the High Street, Chipping Ongar. Turn left. Crowded around the Budworth Hall clocktower is a cafe, toilets, library, and pedestrian crossing: go through the car park beside the Cock Inn on to a waymarked permissive path by the 12th century Motte. At Castle Farm, turn left along a fenced headland, then follow a diversion down to the riverbank. Turn left, upstream, to a footbridge. Cross and continue upstream, then go over a cartbridge at a confluence and ascend to pass to the right of High Ongar's school and the Red Lion Inn to reach Mill Lane. Turn left to St Mary's Church, then right to the Foresters' Arms. Turn left along a fenced path just before the inn crossing a field by a pole to a stiled crossing of the A414.

Follow a path to the south-west corner of the West Park trees, staying to the left until near Pole 33 where a concrete drive is joined. Follow this to The Lodge. The concrete becomes stony and veers off to Little Forest Hall Cottage: continue ahead, joining the track again later and continuing past Little Forest Hall, to the right. At the track's end, a re-instated line goes across to the upper side of the next stand of trees and continues to a gap in the convex corner of a high hedge. The handrail of Tun Bridge is in view, but there is a less visible cartbridge to be crossed just before Tun is reached. Cross the Roding at Tun Bridge and turn downstream, following a waymarked path along the riverbank. Cross each stream draining into the Roding by **footbridge**, following the path to the southern end of Clark's Springs. Here the path emerges from woodland on both banks of the river after crossing a quick succession of sleeper bridges. Go over a stile, and follow a path to a stile by the cottage garden near the start.

POINTS OF INTEREST:
Footbridge – Modifications to rights of way do occur. The final section of this walk, beside the River Roding, has been re-routed to follow the lip of the river bank. Our ancestors left our heritage paths as shown on the Pathfinder map. These paths avoided the likely swampy places and stayed on a line just above the water-table through what were probably woodlands or cleared pastures. Today, thanks to modern land-drainage techiques and subsidies there are less swamps, the land is arable, and the enterprising Essex County Council Ways Through Essex team has added a sturdy footbridge at each confluence, to allow the modification to the current line.

REFRESHMENTS:
The Cock Tavern, Chipping Ongar.
The Foresters' Arms, High Ongar.
The Red Lion, High Ongar.

Maps: OS Sheets Landranger 168; Pathfinder 1100.
The power and the glory of Bradwell juxta Mare.
Start: At 020077, verge parking on Eastend Road, Bradwell-on-Sea.

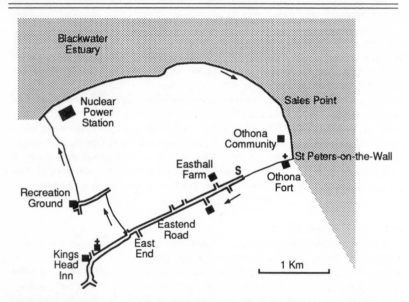

Walk back towards the church in **Bradwell**, passing the Cricketers' Inn and turning right at East End along a concrete road to an ordinary road. Turn left as far as the playground, then right to head NNW with a hedge on the right. Swap to the left of the hedge to reach another concrete track, following it to a stile on to the seawall. Turn right, passing the **Nuclear Power Station**, using the elevated path to reach the bird hides of St Peter's Mudflats. Ever more of the ecologically important land fringing this coast is acquiring protection under conservation terms.

Round the tip of the Dengie peninsula, bringing a bird hide on stilts in to view. On the landward side lives the Christian Community of Othona. As the wall-top path steps down a level, so **St Peter-on-the-Wall Church** is revealed in close-up, a sublime spot, as yet untarnished by internal combustion engines. Close by is the site of the **Roman Fort** of Othona. A grassy agricultural track now leads inland (WSW) back to the start.

POINTS OF INTEREST:

Bradwell – An airfield was hastily constructed here during World War II, too late for the Battle of Britain, but in good time to be in the thick of things later. The nearby inter-tidal zone was mercilessly exploited as a bombing range.

Nuclear Power Station – Electricity for the national grid has been produced at Bradwell's nuclear power station since 1963. Originally intended for twenty years of service, it is still operational. Work began here in 1957, making Bradwell one of the first such stations in the Kingdom.

St Peter-on-the-Wall Church – The Roman occupation ceased after 400 years, and a century or so later Bishop Cedd built a church on the foundations of their fort, one of the first churches in the land. After the Norman conquest, the church became a barn. Forgotten by generations, many now travel on an annual pilgrimage here.

Roman Fort – The Romans built the fort of Othona, set strategically on the Dengie peninsula beside an estuary then known as Panta, in about the 3rd century AD. It was the only one they built on the 'Saxon Shore' of Essex.

REFRESHMENTS:

The Cricketers' Inn, Bradwell-on-Sea (closed at present, but may re-open).
The Kings Head, Bradwell-on-Sea.

Walk 60   HEYBRIDGE BASIN   5m (8km)

Maps: OS Sheets Landranger 168, Pathfinder 1123.

Where herons fish in narrow fleets amid the muddy ooze.

Start: At 870070, Daisy Meadow Car Park, Heybridge.

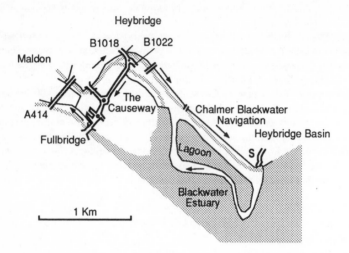

Mount the canal towpath, going left by the Basin and crossing one of the lockgates to get to the side nearer Maldon. Join the seawall path, an isthmus twisting like an escaped eel's mark, around to Maldon, going between the Blackwater and the flooded inland former gravel workings. At high tide the Blackwater is a broad stretch of water brimming to the top of the walls, contrasting with the uncovered view of waders feeding off the ooze at low tide, when herons fish the narrow, remnant fleets of water. The seawall path ends at the dam constructed across the Blackwater after the great floods of 1953. Cross the dam and turn right on the farther bank from St Andrew's Church, to walk beside the relatively dry course of the river. Go around a yard to reach Hey Bridge at the junction of the B1018 and B1022 roads.

Use the sidewalk left of The Causeway, an ancient route across the estuary, to reach **Fullbridge** at the foot of Market Hill, **Maldon**, where the Welcome Sailor is closeted close to the riverbank. Path 11 now goes east and north of the inn to join the seawall of the Chelmer. Follow the wall inland until you are beyond the supermarket fencing. Now leave the seawall and follow the boundary to the canal towpath. Turn left, passing under the A414 to reach a footbridge over the canal. Go back under the road bridge, now on the Heybridge side of the water and follow the **towpath** through Heybridge to return to Heybridge Basin.

POINTS OF INTEREST

Fullbridge –The red hills around the edges of the Blackwater estuary show where the Romans and their followers evaporated seawater to obtain salt. Today the Maldon Crystal Salt Company, near Fullbridge, produces salt by evaporation from a saline extract. The product is in high demand, being an unusally pure sodium chloride, and much of it is exported. At spring tides river water is taken into a reservoir where it is left to settle. It then passes through a complicated filtration process. The simmering lasts for about 48 hours to reveal great drifts of white crystals, with the biggest and best being the last to form.

Maldon – The town celebrated the millennium of *The Song of Maldon* in 1991. The effort galvanised the town, especially the museums. The embroidery is displayed still in the Moot Hall. This is well worth seeing.

Towpath – The return section of the walk passes an industrial zone behind St Andrew's Church in Heybridge. This is the former site of E H Bentall & Company, an agricultural manufacturer well-known before World War II. Elm Farm Dig, the 1994 archaeological site alongside the canal in Heybridge has revealed the sites of three successive townships dating from the Iron Age, the Romano-British period and the Saxon times.

REFRESHMENTS

The Welcome Sailor, Fullbridge.
The Jolly Sailor, Heybridge Basin.
The Old Ship, Heybridge Basin.
Tesco in Fullbridge has a coffee shop and there are numerous possibilities in Maldon.

CASTLE HEDINGHAM   5m (8km)
                                             or 7m (11km)

Maps: OS Sheets Landranger 155 and 167; Pathfinder 1051.
In the verdant upper Colne valley.
Start: At 783342, Summerfields Car Park, Sible Hedingham.

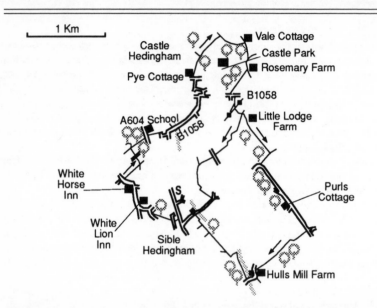

Summerfields is situated opposite the petrol station in Swan Street (the A604). The car park is behind the Co-op supermarket's car park.

Walk along Swan Street towards Halstead as far as Clifton House Surgery and turn right up a path to 15 Colne Road. There. take a north-westerly, tree-lined path, passing the conveniences to join Recreation Road by Gibson Road. Turn left along Alexandra Road to Church Street. Turn right, passing the White Lion and White Horse Inns, and go into St Peter's churchyard. Take either path as they join at a stile by the cemetery extension. Cross the ensuing open space to the northern corner and turn left along a path by garden fences, crossing a road to reach Oxford Lane. Turn right to reach the A604 (Yeldham Road). Cross, with care, and follow a tarmac path beside the school down to Christmas Field. Now bear left and follow Station Road (the

B1058) over the River Colne and into Castle Hedingham. Swap sides of the road when speed is restricted to 30 mph and round the bend by the Wheatsheaf Inn. Use King Street, by the church gate, to enter Falcon Square and swing left to Churchponds. Crown Street now provides the link with Pye Corner, and the path beside Pye Cottage starts the journey around Castle Park. Go over a stile above Churchfield Grove and stay on the right-hand side of a hedged bank on the mid-meadow climb to Rushley Green. Turn right, by Yeomans, following Rosemary Lane as far as Rosemary Farm. There, fork right along a field-edge path which slopes through woodland and passes a cricket field to emerge on St James' Street (the B1058). Turn left, uphill, until opposite the New Park back-garden fences where steps on the right give access to a path by the upper fence-line. Follow the fence until close to overhead wires, then fork left on the mid-field path by a pole and a significant oak tree aligned with Little Lodge Farm to reach a stile in to a Premium Countryside Scheme meadow.

The shorter route does not cross the stile: instead, turn right and follow the left-hand boundary to Sheepcot Lane. Cross and take Maiden Ley Farm drive opposite. Swing left through the nursery cloches and pass to the south side of the piggery fence beyond. Go over a footbridge into a meadow beside an old railway line. Go left, uphill, to reach a road (Alderford Street) beside the railway bridge parapets. Go right, passing the pumps either side of Alderford Mill to rejoin the longer route.

The longer walk crosses the stile into the Premium meadow. Go just below the farmhouse to follow the right-hand fence through the next field, joining a headland by the woodland corner. Continue south-eastwards to join a Great Maplestead bridleway from Hosden's Farm. Go right, then left on Purls Hill Road. Follow the road to a junction on the left by a red letter box. Here, re-enter the Colne Valley by turning right along Path 23, following the right-hand hedge as far as the water valve, and then the chestnut paling fence down to a stile. Go over and continue, going over the old railway track and into Hull's Mill Farmyard. Here, a high double gate appears to block the way, but a gap is waymarked by the cypress foliage to its right. Go left along a road and round the mill to the ford. The footbridge railings also act as a stile for Sible Hedingham Path 57: turn right along this, staying riverside until a fence ushers the path a field's width away from the Colne. Now use the well-worn path parallel with the valley floor to reach a road at Alderford Mill. Turn left, rejoining the shorter route.

Go along the road to its T-junction with Swan Street. Turn right back to the start.

REFRESHMENTS:
There are numerous possibilities in Castle Hedingham and Sible Hedingham, including those mentioned in the text.

Walk 63   STOCK   5m (8km)

Maps: OS Sheets Landranger 167; Pathfinder 1142.
Tree-lined paths and lanes by Stock Harvard.
Start: At 687987, Stock Harvard church.

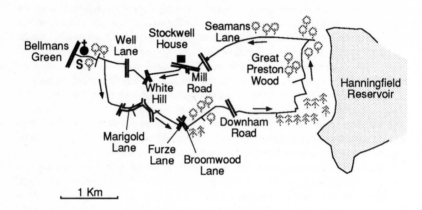

Go through the churchyard on the paved route veering from the porch by the George VI raised octagonal monument to reach the hedge end. Go through the eastern gate into a meadow. Cross a bridge into an open shrubby area and climb to a kissing gate. Go through and continue eastwards to a stile south of a white wooden cottage. Go over and follow a meadow path southwards, continuing along the left-hand hedge of the next meadow. Swing left by a pond to reach a road by Pilgrims Farm. Turn right, then almost immediately left into Marigold Lane. At its end, turn right along Peter Street and where the tarmac ceases, turn sharp left. Go over a stile and follow the right-hand hedge through two grazing plots to reach Furze Lane. Turn left, and right at the cross-roads into Broomwood Lane. At the end of the woodland on the left, turn left along Kiln Common Lane, signed to Rosebery and Bluebell Cottage. Where the lane bends to Bluebell Cottage, go straight ahead to reach a stile. Cross the rough grazing beyond, going under wires to reach a stile on to Downham Road. Turn right to the white railings of a bridge, and there turn left over a stile and follow a brook downstream towards **Hanningfield Reservoir**. Good headlands skirt the fields to the conifer screen around the water.

Now follow white topped waymarker posts northwards from the trees to a bend in the left-hand hedgerow. Cross a field to the corner of some fir trees. Turn northwards again to reach a T-junction of paths. Go right, bearing left to cross a stiled bridge. Continue northwards along a re-instated path to reach a footbridge on the east side of Great Preston Wood. Cross and follow a path heading NNE across a field to a cartbridge by the reservoir hedge. Follow the hedge to the gate before the woodland and go through on to Seamans Lane. Turn left along Seamans Lane, which could easily be renamed Seatmans Lane because of the seats along its shady verges. The lane is a bridleway designated as 'A Country Promenade' suitable for wheelchairs. Go through the gate by Corner Cottage, cross a road and follow the path opposite to **Mill Lane**. Turn right, passing the Stock village nameplate and a red letterbox to reach a footpath on the left, opposite Stockwell House. Fences and hedges steer this path to a hydrant on White Hill. Turn left, pass the front of Sil Jan, left, and turn right along Madles Lane as far as the shed in the left-hand garden. A path to the right here enters the garden of a thatched cottage. Go over an improvised stile into the rough paddock west of the garden. Cross diagonally to its north-west exit and let the fencing steer you through a young plantation and between gardens to Well Lane. Turn right, passing No. 25, right, and turning left after No. 32 along a path that runs parallel with Sunnybrook Farm drive. Drop to a bridge, cross and climb a banked path to pass the white timbered cottage encountered on the outward route. Now retrace the outward route back to the start.

POINTS OF INTEREST:

Hanningfield Reservoir – The reservoir was built 1952-56 and covers some 350 hectares. Under the water are many former homes of great farming families. Today some access for fishing, ornithology, and board sailing is permitted.

Mill Lane – Stock windmill, just visible near the junction of Mill Lane and Mill Road is open to the public on certain summer Sunday afternoons. Admission is free. It is a tower type mill, the only survivor of three mills – the other two were post types – which once operated on this lofty site.

REFRESHMENTS:

There are several possibilities in Stock.

Walk 64   **TOLLESBURY**   5m (8km)

Maps: OS Sheets Landranger 168; Pathfinder 1099 and 1123.
Especially good at dawn or dusk.
Start: At 963106, Woodrolfe Green car park, Tollesbury.

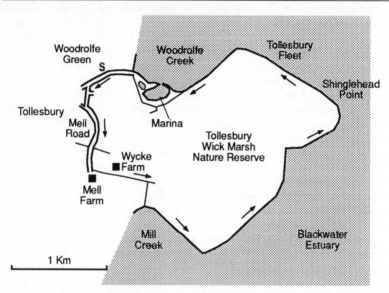

Go over the old railway hump and turn left along Crescent Road to reach Mell Road.
Go left again, all the way to Mell Farm's gate. Beside it is a kissing gate: go through
on to a short, shady path and follow it to the major farm track, go ahead along that
down to the marshland level. Near the bottom, 'Private' signs are designed to avoid
overshooting the right turn. Turn right along the right-hand hedge, before the octagonal
tower is reached, and walk to the seawall. Mount it slowly to see the birds before a
redshank gives an alarm call. Go left along the elevated walk to the corner of Mill
Creek, by the course of the former railway pier which extended to the deepest water
in mid-channel. The whitish water tank seen over Osea Island up the estuary is at
Cold Norton about 6 miles away.

    Continue towards Shinglehead Point with the cuboids of Bradwell Power Station
over the Blackwater to the right. An old defensive pillbox makes a seat at a vantage

site by the Spit. Compounds of mud-coated wickerwork on the seaward side of the wall are intended to save the saltings from erosion. Sheep stray seaward off the wall grazing to vary their diet with samphire and grasses tough enough to survive diurnal saltwater drenchings. Yellow horned poppies, thrift and sea lavender delight with their colour in this area where the sea persistently reflects the mood of the sky. Continue along the wall alongside Tollesbury Fleet with the two Cobb Islands barely poking above high water. The housing on an island way beyond the saltings is at West Mersea. Inland, Tollesbury Wick Marshes have been acquired as a **nature reserve**. Stock grazing is part of the management plan to re-create habitats once known to support small mammals and their predators. Watch for owls, harriers and other raptors, and for herons.

The wall bends in by Woodrolfe Creek to reach the ancient haven of Tollesbury at the Hard. Here is the heart of the village's boat building, fishing and old oyster enterprises. Pass the **marina** and round the wall by the open-air swimming pool to join the road by the stilted sail-lofts. Pass through the Woodrolfe Business area to refind the car park by the conveniences.

POINTS OF INTEREST:

Nature Reserve – The Essex coast has been an ESA (Environmentally Sensitive Area) since 1993, a victory for the tireless efforts of wildlife trust workers in organisations like the Royal Society for the Protection of Birds who negotiated with each other, landowners and farmers to create grasslands suitable for migrating birds.

Marina – How many masts poked skyward from the marina when you walked by? Try to imagine 117 fishing smacks mud-berthed around the Hard before the marina was constructed, for that is the estimated size of the fleet working from Woodrolfe at the beginning of this century. Some dredged, others trawled, to land a variety of seafood at Tollesbury. Crabs and winkles provided the local railway with its name. To these could be added specialities like oysters, sprats, starfish (caught for sale as manure), scallops and hoppers or dabs.

The smacks, depending upon mainsail, foresail and jib for motion and muscle for hauling in the nets, were away for about ten days and would return with a catch of up to six tons. The crew would have a stake in the revenue and relied upon the whims of market forces to price a reward for their labours.

REFRESHMENTS:

There are excellent inns in Tollesbury and a cafe in the Woodrolfe Business Area.

Maps: OS Sheets Landranger 168; Pathfinder 1123.
A walk by a church of rural discovery.
Start: At 993037, Tillingham Recreation Ground.

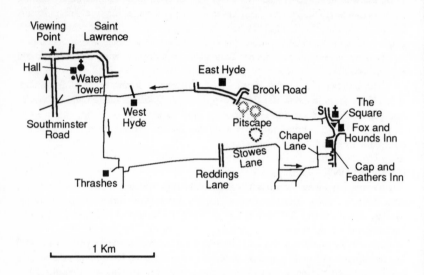

Walk westwards from the conveniences, going along the northern edge of the recreation
ground and through its western exit. Now walk with a ditch on your right to reach a
bridge that allows the path to follow the opposite lip. At a junction of ditches another
bridge allows the crossing of a headland and a resumption of walking with a ditch on
your right-hand side. Go past a tree-lined pitscape to reach a three-way road junction.

    Maintain direction, going ahead again at the first, sharp right, bend into a field.
Follow the left-hand hedge, crossing West Hyde drive to reach a re-instated mid-field
path that leads just left of the water tower silhouette. At the western edge of the large
field is a footbridge. Continue past newly planted trees. Now follow a re-instated path
to reach the double signposts on Southminster Road. Turn right to reach the beacon
post overlooking Stone Point and St Lawrence Bay. Now head eastwards along the
ridge road, passing **St Lawrence Church** and going around the right-hand section of

a Z-bend. On the left-hand section, bear right to walk ahead along a bridleway to return to the footbridge reached earlier.

Now head southwards along the bridleway, which has been diverted to the western hedgeline. Bend left and right as far as a pylon where an east-west track crosses from Thrashes. Turn left to a field edge, going southwards for a few steps before stepping on the next field to the east. Follow the left-hand hedge on a path with an ever-improving surface to reach Reddings Lane. Go left, and then right along unmade Stowes Lane. This leads past award-winning pitscapes to a farmyard. Turn right at the farmhouse, going along a track which bridges over to the next field.

Follow a well-worn path along the left-hand boundary, crossing the northern lip of a ditch and bearing round left to reach the western end of Chapel Lane. Turn right along the lane to reach the Wayside Pulpit on the B1021. Turn left, passing the Cap and Feathers Inn to reach The Square, **Tillingham**, dominated by St Nicholas' Church. From here it is just a step back to the start.

POINTS OF INTEREST:

St Lawrence Church – The Church of St Lawrence Newland is first recorded in 1189 in connection with Beeleigh Abbey's Charter. The present, 1878, building remains a church for worship as well as a frequent venue for the Church of Rural Discovery Exhibitions. The Rural Discovery Church has summer weekend openings of exhibitions related to local history, natural history, historic buildings, farming and wildlife, footpaths and much more.

Tillingham – There is early evidence of Tillingham's history in the form of documents relating to land agreements with St Paul's London in 616 AD. Today it is just the sort of average-sized attractive village to inspire some hope for those campaigning to maintain and improve mainstream services in rural communities. It has been selected by the Rural Community Council for a pilot project to help the survival of remote rural villages as communities.

REFRESHMENTS:
The Cap & Feathers, South Street, Tillingham.
The Fox & Hounds, The Square, Tillingham.

Walk 66　　　　　TOPPESFIELD　　　　　5m (8km)

Maps: OS Sheets Landranger 155; Pathfinder 1051.
Beside a headwater of the Colne River catchment.
Start: At 740375, Church Lane, Toppesfield.

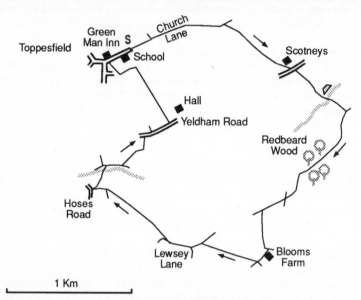

Walk along Church Lane, **Topplesfield** away from the Green Man Inn, passing the school. Continue along an unmade section of the lane, with splendid views over the Stambourne Brook and **River Colne** valleys to the north. Beyond the last, lonely dwelling the lane reduces to bridleway proportions and serpentines gently through thorny growth before widening again prior to reaching a road by Scotneys. Cross the road and go through the bricked gateway of the dwelling opposite. Follow the left-hand hedge down to the valley of Toppesfield Brook. Skirt the lagoons and follow yellow waymarks to cross a footbridge. Ignore the path going right: instead, climb the valley side to reach a path junction by an orchard. Go right along a bridleway, passing Redbeard Wood and contouring the valley before climbing by the airstrip to join a lane by Blooms Farm.

Turn right for about 200 yards, then turn right again, leaving the lane along a bridleway dropping into the valley. Follow the left-hand hedge down, then step over a ditch. Climb the valley side by a fringe of trees to join Lewsey Lane. Turn right for about 200 yards to where the lane begins to pull out of the valley. Here a path continues ahead, contouring the valley beside a hedge. Cross a bridge into the next field and cross parallel with the brook, converging with another path to meet a bend in Hoses Road. From this point turn very sharply right on to another path which crosses the same field, heading north-eastwards to reach a footbridge. Cross and turn right along a lane servicing the sewerage treatment plant. Pass to the left of the plant and cross a small field to a footbridge by the bend of a bank. Cross and go under power cables. Now walk to the convex hedge corner and use a re-instated path to reach a road. Turn right and take the second fieldpath on the left, before Toppesfield Hall is reached. Make for the hedge end and follow the boundary around until you are south of the church. Now cross a footbridge and head towards the church's south porch. Bear left to rejoin Church Lane.

POINTS OF INTEREST:

Topplesfield – This is a good example of a nucleated village. Settled on the northern bank of the Brook, Toppesfield gathers itself charmingly round the 14th-century St Margaret of Antioch Church. Beneath its dominating red brick tower of 1699 is an ideal rural scene: a working school, a memorial to one generation of young men, followed by the young men of the next generation sacrificed in two World Wars, a roofed pump with seat doubling as a bus stop. The Green Man survives as the village pub – its neighbourly rival across The Street is now a private dwelling.

The playing field huddles close by, and surrounding all is a huge arable acreage spread across the rolling countryside, laced throughout by the all-important public footpaths.

River Colne – This is not the only river so named in England. It rises in Essex by Moyns Park in Steeple Bumpstead and crosses some 30 miles of the county to reach Colchester at the tidal limit of a long estuary which joins the North Sea by Lee-over-Sands. A short river with a mere 320 foot fall, it was expected to work hard for its passage by turning the many waterwheels located at frequent intervals from Hedingham to Colchester.

REFRESHMENTS:
The Green Man Inn, Toppesfield.

Maps: OS Sheets Landranger 169; Pathfinder 1078.
By the barge quays of Hamford Water.
Start: At 187234, a lay-by on the B1414 north of Thorpe le Soken.

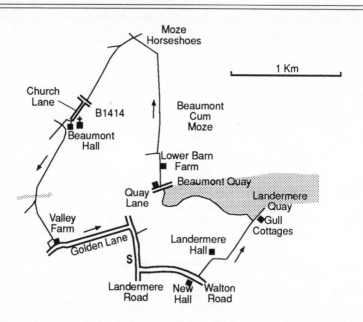

There are lay-bys either side of the road between the Walton Road and Golden Lane junctions.

Walk eastwards along the Walton Road as far as New Hall, on the right, then turn left along Landermere Lane, passing Landermere Hall on the way to Landermere Quay. The first buildings there are Gull Cottages, named not for the seabirds, but in recognition of a former occupant, as the brass plate reveals. From the water's edge return to the arable edge in front of Gull Cottages and walk along the hedge to the seawall. Follow this elevated walk around the derelict sea transport abandoned in tidal rills, to reach Quay Farm in **Beaumont-cum-Moze**. Cross Quay Lane and follow a track to, and beyond, Lower Farm. Notices rightly preclude unauthorised entry to the buildings and their livestock. Authentic walkers stay on the right-of-way which continues off the track-bend, staying right of the hedge stretching northward across the flat valley of Hamford. At the hedge junction, go over the stile in the thicker hedge and cross a grazing plot. A matching stile returns the path to arable land.

The climb out of the valley soon steepens: cross an arable field to its north-west corner and climb beside the right-hand hedge to a cross-paths at Moze Horseshoes. Turn left across the same arable field to a hedge corner and use the track on the left of the hedgerow to reach the B1414. Cross into Church Lane opposite and pause to admire **St Leonard's and St Mary's Church**, another in the range of fine small churches to be found in Essex. Now walk towards Beaumont Hall, but go to the far right of the drive and through a gap in the quadrangle corner to reach an arable landscape stretching across to Tendring. Go left, behind the Hall, and then right to follow the right-hand hedge down and across two fields to reach the valley's stream. Cross a cartbridge and turn right. Now swing left and up beside a hedgerow to reach the back of Valley Farm. Move to the right-hand field and follow its edge to reach a gap on to Golden Lane. Turn left along the lane to its T-junction with the B1414. To the right is the starting lay-by.

POINTS OF INTEREST:

Beaumont-cum-Moze – Agricultural advances in Essex during the 18th century were reflected at Beaumont. They were pursued by established landowners such as Lord Bramston at Skreens, by some newer landowners such as Lord Western at Rivenhall, and by some glebe-managing clergy at Beaumont. The implications of the improving husbandry included both population and employment increases. At Beaumont it set the pattern, and surrounding landowners attempted to match it, thus increasing the tithe payable to the parish.

St Leonard's and St Mary's Church – Lord Byng is associated with the church where he was known to quietly worship away from the trappings of the high distinction he earned in his everyday work. He was a commander at Vimy Ridge in World War I, leading Canadian forces to victory. After the war he served as Governor-General of Canada before returning to become Chief Commissioner of London Police.

REFRESHMENTS:
None on the route, but there are several excellent possibilities in nearby Thorpe-le-Soken.

HADSTOCK   5m (8km)

Maps: OS Sheets Landranger 154; Pathfinder 1027.
Range free on rolling chalk and tree quilted countryside.
Start: At 575450 verge parking on Bartlow Road, Hadstock.

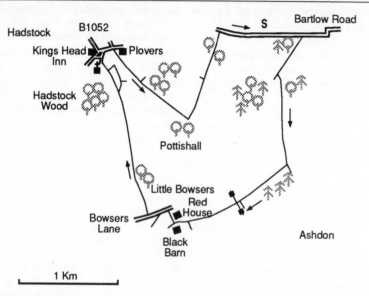

Walk towards **Bartlow** and turn right along the unmade road by the corner of a spinney, about 150 yards short of the buttressesof the former railway bridge. Climb the track beyond the spinney and a quarry, then fork left to enter Ashdon before 33 Acre Covert is reached. The unmade road crests a rise by a belt of pine trees stretching down to the River Bourne valley, and dips, a field away from a red-roofed, renovated dwelling established by the former railway track. As the next rise begins, a bridleway is waymarked to the right, by a conifer plantation. Take this, climbing at first, then dipping beyond the trees. Cross the junction with a footpath and continue to join a concrete drive which approaches a black barn at Bowsers End. Turn right with the drive to pass The Red House and reach Bowsers Lane. Go left, as waymarked, to just beyond Little Bowsers Nursery. Here waymarkers point right along a field-edge. Climb along a mid-field path to reach a spinney. The path goes beside a ditch to the crest of the hill, then continues mid-field. Cross several bridges over ditches draining right to the Bourne before Hadstock and Hadstock Wood come into view. Overhead wires converge from the right and enter the north-east corner of the small field north of the woodland: head for a bridge mid-way between the wood and a pole carrying wires across the valley. Now follow waymarkers away from the mapped route by the mid-field row of trees, to the right-hand edge, by the ivy-clad tree. Further waymarkers follow the right-hand hedge round a concave corner to reach a stile beneath the wires, just one paddock away from the church and village hall. Cross the paddock by the transformer station to reach St Botolph's Church, **Hadstock**. Leave the churchyard NNE by Beam Ends and go down to Church Green. Go up Bartlow Road to Hillcrest Cottage opposite Moules Lane. The path heading south-eastwards behind Plovers is not easy to negotiate, the hedges are overgrown and the surface ruptured by an overload of hooves. Follow the path until overhead wires are met by a spinney. Turn left on to a gravelled track leading northwards between other stands of trees, near or one field away, and follow it to Bartlow Road. Turn right to return to the start.

POINTS OF INTEREST:

Bartlow - Bartlow Hills, at 586449 south-east of the village, are ancient monuments, rated by some to among the best Romano-British tombs in the land. Once there were seven hills, now reduced to a visible three, with a fourth said to be hidden. Much of what was discovered in the tombs was destroyed by fire in a new, less-safe keeping place. Some material remains in Cambridge and Saffron Walden museums. The hills are best approached on foot from the south-east corner of Bartlow churchyard.

Hadstock - The village has a charter, dated 1129, for a market on St Botolph's Day to accompany the fair known to have been held in the year of King Edward (the Confessor's) death. The charter, emanating from King Henry when in Rouen, and issued to Bishop Hervey of Ely, is held in Ely Cathedral.

REFRESHMENTS:

The Kings Head, Hadstock.
There are also possibilities in Bartlow and Ashdon.

Walk 69   **ABBERTON**   5m (8km)

Maps: OS Sheets Landranger 168; Pathfinders 1076, 1099 and 1100.

In Roman River valley and reservoir countryside

Start: At 005183, a lay-by on Pete Tye Common, near Abberton.

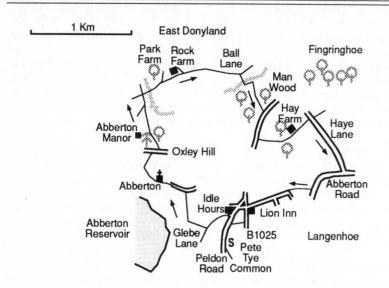

Follow the road (Peldon Road) up towards Abberton as far as Idle Hours, then turn left along unmade Glebe Lane. Pass the water tower, and where the right-hand hedge gives way to an arable field, turn right on the field-edge path towards **Abberton Reservoir**. This footpath is open to the public only during daylight hours 364 days a year: on the first Monday of each year it is closed. As the path steepens, go over a stile at a right-hand hedge junction and walk beside the hedge to reach a stile on Rectory Lane. Turn left towards St Andrew's Church, going over two stiles to cross a farm approach, to reach the churchyard's ornamental gates. Go through and walk to a gate north of the tower. Cross the grazing beyond north-westwards to a concave bend around an arable field, and veer to a stile on to Oxley Hill. Turn right to the crest of the hill and there turn left along Path 4, alongside Abberton Manor. Follow the path through a triangle of wilderness, passing closer to the stand of white poplar saplings than the tall cedar tree, to reach a stile. Across the Roman River valley a black pipeline may be seen arching over the waterway. Left of it is a metallic gate: head for that gated crossing of Layer Brook. Go over a stile to reach a junction of paths at the confluence of the brook with the river beside a bridle-bridge to the right.

Cross to Donyland and climb a track to an upper stile. Go over and walk straight ahead on the lesser path, by the right-hand hedge, to the Rock Farm compound. Join Ball Lane by a stand of teasels and follow through to its first left bend. Beside the right-hand passing bay, there is a stile: go over and take the shortest route to the Roman River footbridge. On the Langenhoe side, turn downstream for one field, then walk beside the hedge to a stile in the lower woodland fence. Go over and follow a path through Man Wood to a stile on to the B1025. Go over and turn right, uphill, with care, to the oak tree beyond the village sign. Go left on a mid-field path, passing an oak tree to reach steps and a stile under another oak tree. A footbridge of concrete joists under an adjacent field maple tree, leads to a narrow field. Cross and go over the upper stile on to a track that leads by Hay Farm to reach a stony drive to Haye Lane. Turn right, uphill, to a T-junction. Turn right along Abberton Road, turning right, off it, by Grange Bungalow, opposite the yellow hydrant marker. Follow a fenced and hedged path to the '40' speed sign on Fingringhoe Road. Walk ahead to a cross-roads, where the Lion Inn will be found to the left. Turn left, past the inn, following the Mersea Road for 200 yards to reach a yellow hydrant marker just beyond Uppershott. Turn right, crossing the road to reach a field-edge path that is followed to Peldon Road. Turn left, downhill, to the start.

POINTS OF INTEREST:

Abberton Reservoir – The reservoir enjoys a world-wide reputation as a bird haven. The more waders and other birds are attracted to the environs, the more bird-watchers arrive to scrutinise them. There is a visitor centre on the B1026 causeway across the water.

Migrant birds have no need for man's boundaries. For them the environs of the reservoir extend to the Roman River Valley Conservation Zone, to the military training zones by Donyland Heath and Fingringhoe Ranges, to the grasses of Pete Tye Common and over to the National Nature Reserves around the nearby estuaries.

REFRESHMENTS:
The Lion Inn, Langenhoe.

Maps: OS Sheets Landranger 167, Pathfinder 1075.
From Finchingfield, the most photographed village in the county.
Start; At 683326, Stephen Marshall Avenue, Finchingfield.

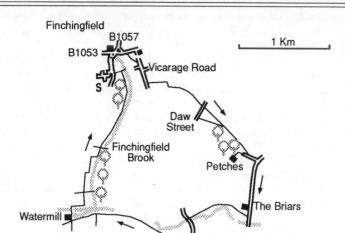

Walk to the Post Office, turn left and veer towards the pond. Cross the pond's outfall
bridge and swing right, uphill, to pass the Finch Inn. Opposite the Red Lion go through
the opening by the 15th-century Guildhall to join a path that crosses St John's
churchyard to reach Vicarage Road. Pass the school to reach the speed de-restriction
signs, forking left there along Path 11. Follow the left-hand hedge to steps and go up
to the higher field level. Continue along a mid-field path with glorious views to
Wethersfield and the Pant valley. Cross Daw Street, continuing to a bridge by the
copse. Cross and climb a track, going under the cables to reach a lane where Petches'
drive joins it. Go ahead, along the lane, to a junction and turn right, downhill. Go past
The Briars, then turn right along Path 13, between the chain-link fences of the Treatment
Compounds. From the western corner go mid-field to a raised inspection cover and
then cross to the bank of the Pant. Walk beside the river, going over a plank bridge

into the next field where the path alternates from riverside to mid-field as the Pant meanders. Continue to reach Daw Street by Sculpin's neat and tidy bridge. Turn left, cross the river and follow the lane until you are level with the valley pillbox in the field to the left. Opposite is a waymarked gateway hidden in the thick hedge. Go through to a stile on to grassland. Head westwards to a concrete bridge and gate into a riverside pasture. Near the far corner, by another river meander, is a double stile to further grazing. Cross to a bridge/stile.

Cross and continue along the valley, but not on the river bank, to reach a gate at a corner (grid ref. 685311). Go through and continue over a mid-field bridge to reach the far hedge. A broken and barbed gate guards against progress to the north of the compound, but another gate offers an alternative to the south: stay close to the Great Bardfield Watermill stream to reach a corner by a pond. Go through a hedge gap and walk to the Millhouse. Turn right by the wheelhouse ruins and cross a short meadow to the Pant footbridge. Follow the river downstream to the field corner and bear left by the hedge to reach Champion's drive. Cross this to a stile into linked paddocks. Cross the first and use a concrete block as a stile to reach the second. Cross to a stile, go over and turn right to reach Path 38. Follow the path along Finchingfield Brook, heading upstream through fields, garden paddocks, snowberry clumps and orchards until the path diverges from the brook under a stand of thorn trees. Now walk along garden fencing to reach a T-junction with Path 41. Go left to Bardfield Road: Stephen Marshall Avenue is opposite.

POINTS OF INTEREST
The Duck End Mill at Finchingfield has been restored as a visual feature, its white woodwork delighting thousands of tourists. Gibraltar Mill, at nearby Great Bardfield, has been restored and is a visual delight. By contrast, visits cannot be arranged to this tower mill which is now a private residence.

REFRESHMENTS
There are several possibilities in Finchingfield, including those mentioned in the text.

Walk 71   **PODS BROOK VALLEY**   5m (8km)

Maps: OS Sheets Landranger 167; Pathfinder 1075.
Rayne and Panfield guard the young River Brain.
Start: At 726224, Station Road, Rayne.

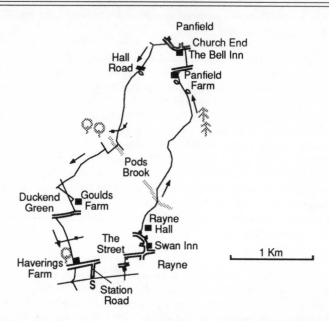

Join the **former railway line,** now a linear open space, and head east for Braintree. Pass the old platform and siding space to find a crossing path by some lock-up garages. Turn left to reach and follow Symmons Close. Go over Medley Road and continue along an urban path to The Street. Turn right, then left along Shalford Road by the traffic lights near the Swan Inn. Pass the war memorial and turn right along a lane between Rayne Hall Farm and a thatched cottage by a hydrant. Descend the lane to bridge Pods Brook. Go along the concrete bridleway beyond, passing the sewage treatment compound and climbing to the hangars of Rayne Hall Farm airstrip. Follow the gravelled track only when conflict with aircraft is unlikely. Ignore side turnings, descending slightly to a cartbridge. Cross and follow a grassed headland beside the trees-in-ditch, right. Go over another cartbridge into a second field. Bear left with the hedge about 70 yards short of the pine tree belt, and from the north-east corner enter a double hedged lane, following it to Panfield Farm. Turn right along Hall Road and turn left beside Laburnum on a path to the village hall at Church End. Turn left to the Bell Inn. Continue along the road, then turn left on a path on the south side of No. 57. The path hugs the back garden fences as far as a bridge by a pole. Do not cross: instead, go left to reach Hall Road again.

Opposite, to the right, is a pond with a transformer on a pole by a field entrance: follow its western edge, continuing back to the valley of Pods Brook. Where the overhead wires leave the hedge, look for a sharp bend of the hedge to the right. Go left from this point to use a cultivation line under the wires midway between two poles, and so locate the parallel bars of a footbridge. Now follow the right-hand hedge for 70 yards to reach a footbridge on the right. Follow the same hedgrerow, but now on the other side, up through a plantation to reach a gravelled lane through arable crops. Where the left-hand ditch is piped under to the right-hand side, the required cross-path begins, but it is diverted around obstructions. Continue up the lane to the next power pole, and go left along the crop edge to a plank bridge in the corner. Continue on a crop-change line towards a cluster of cypress trees by Goulds Farm buildings. Turn right, as indicated by a blacksmithed pointer and follow the garden boundary trees to cross a stile into the garden. Stay on the mown zone inside the western boundary to reach a drive close to Duckend Green. Turn right by Martens, then left by the unlimiting speed signs to follow a green track by the garden hedge. Next, go mid-field under power lines to reach a tree belt at Haverings Farm. Turn left along The Street, as far as the 'Give Way to Oncoming Traffic' sign. Now cross and follow Path 13 along the left-hand hedge to reach the Flitch Way Country Park. Turn left to return to the start.

POINTS OF INTEREST:
Former railway line – This was the link from the east coast main line at Witham to the Kings Lynn line at Bishops Stortford. Passenger services still exist between Witham and Braintree, but post World War II traffic west of Braintree was mainly of sugar beet to the Felsted factory by Little Dunmow station.

REFRESHMENTS:
The Swan Inn, Rayne.
The Bell Inn, Panfield.

Walk 72   **BIRCHANGER**   5m (8km)

Maps: OS Sheets Landranger 167; Pathfinder 1074.

A ringlet by the bright Stort ribbon.

Start: At 511251, Crafton Green Car Park, Stansted Mountfitchet.

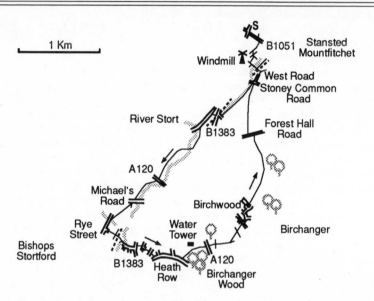

Walk down Chapel Hill beyond the Old Courtroom and turn right on to the Recreation Ground. Follow a surfaced lane as far as the open space and fork left to descend to a crossing of Millside with Woodfields. Ignore both, and Woodfield Close, to select the fifth outlet, a narrow path, following it to Millfields. Go left, downhill, and bridge both Stansted Brook and the railway. Walk parallel to the railway on a path which develops as West Road. Turn right at the end, along Stoney Common Road, as far as the railings around Stansted Brook bridge. Walk downstream through a black gate and keep the brook on your right through the grasses of The Mount to reach the B1383 (Pines Hill) where it crosses the railway. Go down steps by the western parapet and follow a short path to Gypsy Lane. Turn left as far as the confluence of Stansted Brook with the River Stort. There, turn left along a path beside the river, using sleeper bridges to cross two inflowing streams. The path then serpentines around to a girder

138

bridge. Cross into Hertfordshire and follow a path over stiles, following the left-hand fence on to a headland atop a well-burrowed bank. Go under a span of the A120 to reach the river again. Diverge from the river where it passes under Red, White & Blue Road to reach a road by a powerline pole. The road is narrow, so carefully cross to a stile. Go over and head south-westwards to Bourne Brook Bridge. Turn left along Rye Street to reach Cannons Mill Lane on the left.

Descend the lane, cross a railway level crossing, with care, and continue to the B1383 (Stansted Road). Steps beside No. 220 lead over Collins Cross and Lea Green cul-de-sacs to 79 Heath Row. Turn left towards Hockerill water tower. By No. 127 a track, to the left, leads past the tower into Birchanger Wood. Stiles and ramps aid a crossing of the A120 carriageway amid the trees. Continue to a cross-paths to the east of the Wood. Go ahead, following a grassy path which bends left to reach silver birches east of a green barn. Go over a track, and follow a fenced path to Birchwood off Birchanger Lane. Go past the Men's Club and wind left and right twice to reach a path which goes behind No. 67 and between Nos. 59 and 61A. Now follow a broad green path by Parsonage Springs, going to the left of some farm buildings to reach Forest Hall Road. Turn left as far as the end of the field you have just walked, then turn right up a path beside a track to some glasshouses. Pass a house with a large loft-tank and follow hedges down to Stoney Common Road. Now retrace the outward route back to the start in **Stansted Mountfitchet**.

POINTS OF INTEREST:
Stansted Mountfitchet – The town castle has a rebuilt Norman wooden motte and bailey on a site overlooking Stansted Brook, by the station. Richard de Montfitchet was one of the barons who caused Magna Carta to be signed. The site is believed to have been well-used from Iron Age times to 1215. Next to the Castle is a Toy and Doll Museum.
Aeroplanes overhead will probably be using Stansted Airport constructed a decade ago, and still expanding.

REFRESHMENTS:
There are numerous possibilities in Stansted Mountfitchet.

Walks 73 & 74   CHRISHALL   5m (8km)
                                      or $7^1/_2$m (12km)

Maps: OS Sheets Landranger 154; Pathfinder 1050.
Oldfield Grove, at 147 metres the highest land in Essex.
Start: At 460394, Kings Lane Nature Reserve Car Park, Elmdon.

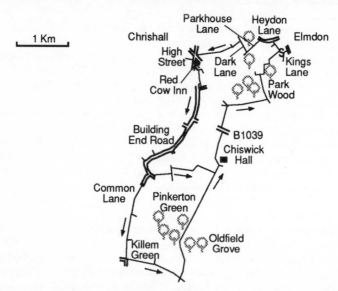

Leave the grassy area beside the eastern hedge, heading NNW over two stiles and a
footbridge to reach Heydon Lane. Go left to the triangular junction. Take the left fork,
an unmade road heading between blocks of woodland, then turn right by the junction
of overhead wires to resume a NNW direction. As the woodside path begins to dip to
a small valley, go over a stile to the left and follow a mid-field path towards Chrishall.
Go over several stiles as you walk westwards through sheep pasture and on towards a
coach-wash gantry. The path passes close to this to reach Chrishall cross-roads. Take
the second left, High Street, then fork left along Hogg's Lane by the Red Cow Inn.
Beyond the last dwelling the lane becomes a grassy headland: follow it down to Chalky
Lane. Go right, then left along Hollow Road. Join, cross, with care, and leave the
B1039, to continue along Building End Road to reach a road fork.

The shorter route goes left here, climbing to pass through the cluster of dwellings around Upper Farm. Continue eastwards off the road end, going over a stile and along a grass track. Follow the right-hand fence over another stile and down to a gate and footbridge. Turn left along a headland, walking downstream beside an incised brook. A curve of the headland, near left and right waymarkers, brings Yew Tree Cottage roof into view. Go right up the incline of a re-instated path, crest the hill and dip to a bridge over the boundary ditch. Cross and continue eastwards along a mid-field path to Chiswick Hall, rejoining the longer route.

The longer route takes the right fork, following Common Lane to Killem Green. Go left from the road's elbow bend, following a field-edge path ESE for 1,000 yards to reach a path junction one field north of Langley church. Go left along a field edge, then follow a path through narrow **Oldfield Grove**. An unmapped belt of trees now points NNE across Pinkerton Green: walk along the edge of these to join a grassy track descending gently to rejoin the shorter route at Chiswick Hall.

Join the drive down to the B1039. Cross left to a footbridge and follow the mid-field path beyond up to Chrishall church. Go right by the church hedge and follow a headland beyond Park Wood corner to reach a vehicular track in the valley. Turn left, climb along another edge of Park Wood, cross a footbridge and go right and left around the edge of Dewberry Grove. Follow waymarkers through by Kings Grove ponds and down a headland to return to the start.

POINTS OF INTEREST:
Oldfield Grove – At 482 feet (147 m) above OD, this is the highest point in Essex.

The Icknield Way Path emblem of a Stone Age flint and bone axe will be seen on some of the waymarkers on these routes. The Icknield Way is one of the most ancient thoroughfares in Britain. The long distance path which follows it links with other ancient walkways at both ends, the Ridgeway at Ivinghoe and Peddars Way at Knettishall Heath.

REFRESHMENTS:
The King's Head Inn, Elmdon, near the start.
The Red Cow Inn, Chrishall.

Walk 75   **HARWICH HARBOUR**   5¹/₂m (9km)

Maps: OS Sheets Landranger 169; Pathfinder 1054.
Harwich's history, steeped in naval activity.
Start: At 262327, St Helen's Green car park, Harwich.

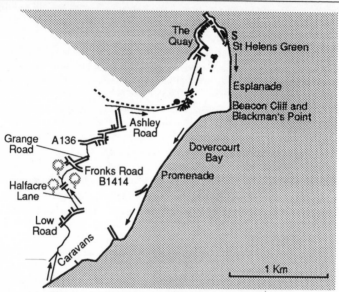

From the start in **Harwich**, walk southwards along the Esplanade. Round Blackmans Point to join the Marine Parade and Promenade of Dovercourt Bay by the earliest east coast lighthouse. Go beyond the last beach hut to the caravan/holiday park. The tarmac path on the seawall gives way to ordinary earth. Cross the first bridge over the borrow dyke after the caravan park and use the midfield path to reach the south-west corner of some holiday homes. Fences steer the lane through to Low Road: turn right as far as Holmleigh. Now turn left on Path 26 which follows the school fencing of Halfacre Lane. Ignore the turning by the school corner, continuing ahead to cross the estate road. Turn right before the community hall on to a path, following it to the Fire and Rescue Station on Fronks Road. Cross the B1414 to Grange Road, following it to reach a footpath beside No. 81. Go north along this to reach the A136 by a hospital. Turn right along the sidewalk, using the pedestrian crossing to reach the Royal Hotel.

Turn left along Princes Road, then go right along Ashley Road and second left along Shaftesbury Avenue. At the northern end of the Avenue a stepped path links right with Harwich Hangings, a footpath by the former railway line before Mr Parkes developed Parkeston Quay. This is a grand viewing point to see beyond Phoenix Bridge which carries the A120 road over both the newer railway, and the old Phoenix Dock of Bathside Bay. Across the Bay is Shotley Point with the white mast kept in place as a reminder of the former HMS Ganges. Annually, on parade day, a cadet would be selected to stand, as button boy, on the top of the mast.

Now merge with a gravelled track and, at a fork with Patrick's Lane, bear left along the railway fence of Station Lane, following it through to Dovercourt Bay Station. Pass the Victoria Hotel to reach a footbridge over the railway from the corner of Station Lane and East Street. From the foot of the steps, fork left on to Stour Road, using the elevated sidewalk as far as the Anchor. Join the A120 road and follow the lorry route's footway around to The Quay and Ha'penny Pier. Finally, use any of the several roads parallel with Kings Quay Street to get back to the car park.

POINTS OF INTEREST:

Harwich – The Harwich Society's enterprise makes a visit to Harwich doubly delightful. To embellish the range of seafaring activities on view, there are plaques and discreet notices erected by the Society to inform and entertain visitors. This facility extends beyond the ten places of outstanding interest on the Town Trail to include smaller items of interest unearthed only after in-depth study. Harwich has had strong Dutch connections since the Mayflower set sail for America in 1620. Harwich was walled and moated with a castle. Its position on an isthmus between Dovercourt and Bathside Bays was very defendable. The town was replanned in the 13th century with a grid system of streets with connecting alleyways. Queen Elizabeth I called it a pretty place that wanted for nothing.

REFRESHMENTS:

There are numerous possibilities in Harwich.

Walk 76   RAMSEY AND GREAT OAKLEY   5¹/₂m (9km)

Maps: OS Sheets Landranger 169, Pathfinder 1053, 1054 and 1078.

By the brook that crumples an edge of Tendring's plain.

Start: At 190310, the Woodland Trust's Stourwood car park.

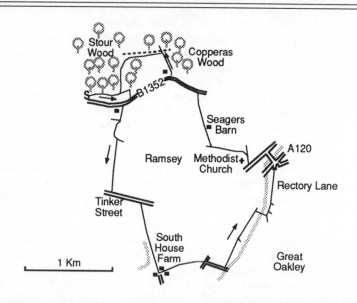

Follow the woodland edge towards Harwich, walking parallel with the road as far as a shed. Fork left, then veer right at the next junction and right again at the eastern edge of the trees to reach a stile on to the B1352. Turn right to Stourwood Nursery and use the bridge and path waymarked along its eastern boundary, to reach a footbridge just beyond the rear garden hedge. Cross and follow a field edge, bearing left into the little valley. Now follow a **path** beside a hedge across three fields to reach Tinker Street, the A120. Turn right along the verge, going downhill, then crossing, with care, to reach a footpath on the right. Follow a midfield path towards the South House Farm buildings on the crest of the hill. Cartbridges give access and exit to the middle field: in the third field keep a ditch on your right-hand side. Turn left through the farm buildings, and use another indistinct midfield path, heading ENE from the newer dwelling, to reach a parish boundary. Bear right by an old hedge and aim for a white post marking Rectory Road's junction with The Soils.

Descend Rectory Road to Saltwater Bridge. Do not cross: instead, go left between paddocks and Ramsey Brook, then follow a brookside path towards Ramsey. Go over two straight-forward stiles, then three which need extra care. Cross two more pastures to a double crossing of wires on poles, then go right under the wires to locate a difficult cradle bridge, crossing it to reach Rectory Lane. Turn left to reach the A120 at a roundabout. Cross, with care, into Ramsey village, following Main Road. Fork left by the Castle Inn and go right between 27 The Street and the Methodist Chapel. Follow a field edge behind the **windmill** to reach a path fork to the north of the mill. Bear left to reach a stile. Go over and cross a field to another stile. Chamfer the corner of the arable field beyond to a stile at a hedge end. Now stay by the high hedge on the right, going over a stile, and exiting over another stile, to the right. Now veer NNW across a field towards Seagers Barn. Pass a pond and follow a track connecting to the B1352. Turn left, towards Wrabness, as far as the Copperas Wood entrance before the white flat-roofed dwelling. Go over a stile on the right and follow the signs along the left-hand hedge as far as a railway bridge. Do not cross: instead, go left over the stiled footbridge of a courtesy footpath which hugs the railway, heading westwards to Stourwood. Go into the wood and follow a blue and yellow waymarked path as it bridges two streams and returns to the car park.

POINTS OF INTEREST:

Windmill – Ramsey Windmill, tall and thin, is built off the crest of the hillside overlooking Ramsey Creek brook. Originally it stood in a similar situation by the River Deben in Suffolk, but was re-assembled on its current site in 1842. It is a private residence, not open to the public.

Path – Ramsey Eight, the footpath used from Stourwood to Tinker Street, is an important link in the network of paths in Tendring district. The path was blocked in places and walkers detoured around the blockages. When some of the farmland was sold, some new owners disliked the unofficial diversions and sought to extinguish their usage. Happily records showed that some ramblers had reported the faults from 1968 onwards, and given the impetus of the 1990 Rights of Way Act, the Diversion Order in force today was confirmed. It pays to report path problems after each walk!

REFRESHMENTS:
The Castle Inn, Ramsey.
The Black Boy, Wrabness.

Walk 77   ALDHAM AND CHAPPEL   5¹/₂m (9km)

Maps: OS Sheets Landranger 168, Pathfinder 1076 and 1077.
Viaduct views from around Hoe Wood.
Start: At 920262, verge parking on Green Lane, Aldham.

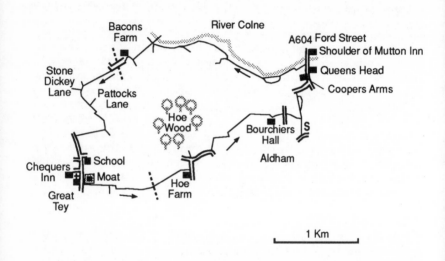

Follow a path northwards from a bend in the lane, going along the left side of the playing field to reach a cross-paths. Continue north, with a hedge on your right to reach New Road. Go right to reach the A604. Turn left along the footway, passing two inns. Just before the Colne bridge, turn left by a dwelling squeezed between the path and the river, then get to the water's edge. Follow Aldham Path 1 along a green headland at the northern edge of arable activity regaining the riverside before becoming Chappel Path 22. Go over stiles and bridges to reach Broom House Bridge, where five paths meet by a World War II pillbox. Select the hedgeside path heading south-westwards up the valley to Bacons Farm. Go between the farm's house and buildings to join Bacons Lane. Follow this over a railway bridge, but where it bends right, continue south-westwards through two fields to reach Stone Dickey Lane. Go left and left again after merging with Pattocks Lane. Follow this to its end. Three steps right

146

transfer the path to a field edge: follow the left-hand hedge into the next field, then turn right along the hedge on the right to reach Chappel Road. Turn left into Great Tey, passing the school, village hall and church.

Turn left on the footpath to the south of a moat. Follow a headland path through fields to reach a brick railway bridge. Now rise with the headland to reach Hoe Farm. Turn left along Rectory Road, heading towards **Hoe Wood**, and right at a T-junction to go along Tey Road. As it bends right, go over a stile and follow the path to the north-east corner gate. Through the gate, follow the railings to a track junction. Continue eastwards, now with more railings on the right, to reach a stile by Bourchiers Hall transformer on stilts. Go over and follow the drive down to New Road. Cross to the headland opposite and follow a hedge to the right to reach a cross-paths by the north-west corner of the recreation ground. Turn right along the outward route to return to the start.

POINTS OF INTEREST:
Hoe Wood – The wood is central to the walk, its trees being in view for most of it. The wood is now owned by The Woodland Trust and is managed under the direction of the local Wildlife Trust. The trees are coppiced on an ongoing cycle, and wildflowers, insects and mammals are encouraged. The wood is open to careful users of the woodland paths, and donations to the Woodland Trust are always welcomed.

REFRESHMENTS:
The Queens Head, Aldham.
The Chequers Inn, Great Tey.
The Swan, Chappel, on the west side of the viaduct.
The Coopers Arms, Adlham on the route.

Maps: OS Sheets Landranger 168, Pathfinder 1076.
In the upper Roman River and Tey Brook valleys.
Start: At 876247, verge parking at Dowsland Green, Great Tey.

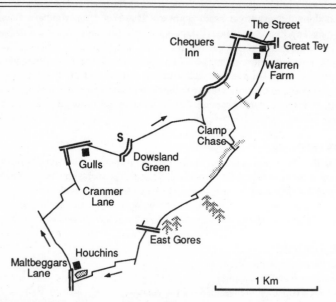

Walk along the lane towards Great Tey and take the first footpath to the right. Follow it across two fields to join Path 31 beside a ditch in the third field. Continue to reach Clamp Chase at a five way junction. Use the Chase, left, to reach a road. Turn right down Coggeshall Road, crossing the Roman River and climbing to a T-junction. Turn right to Great Tey's neatly clustered village centre. Pass Greenfield Drive, and then turn right between The Chequers Inn and St Barnabas Church on a lane that leads to a gate into a meadow. Head for the south-west corner where a waymarked path is cut as a tunnel through the thicket. Cross the concrete drive of Warren Farm and follow a field-side path past the AWA Treatment compound. Cross a bridge over the Roman River by a blue railed outfall. Cross a narrow neck of land to reach a field-edge path which zig-zags twice to join Clamp Chase at a bridge over Tey Brook. Go right, beside the brook for 100 yards, use a double-sleeper bridge over a feeder stream, and continue along the brook to reach a track junction near a belt of conifers. Go left to the north-western end of the belt, then turn right along a headland, passing the next belt of trees to reach a road.

Turn right, downhill, to reach a signed footpath on the left, by a pond, opposite the white metal railings of East Gores Farm. Follow the path (Path 43) to a Y-junction of tracks. Fork right, heading for a hedge with Houchins' chimneys beyond it. At the hedge, chicane left-right to cross a cartbridge. Continue westwards along a headland towards Houchins' reservoir bank. Chicane left-right again to be field-side of the banking and follow the bank's foot to a lane. Turn right, leaving the tarmac to continue northwards, by the fine double jetted **Houchins**, up grassy Maltbeggars Lane. Follow the left hedge, then cross mid-field to reach a short double-hedged section with a cartbridge to the right. Turn right to follow Coggeshall's Path 28 north-eastwards. The path soon becomes Great Tey Path 39: at the field corner, turn left to the first clump of hedging along the boundary. Cross this grassy field divider to use a re-instated path to reach Cranmer Lane. Turn left along the lane, following it to join Buckley Lane. Turn right, passing Gulls Farm to reach a footpath sign, to the left, and a bridleway sign, to the right. Turn right along the bridleway to Dowsland Green, turning left to return to the start.

POINTS OF INTEREST
Houchins – Situated at the southern end of Maltbeggars Lane the house has fine double jetted storeys. It has been admired by travellers along Stane Street for centuries, and more recently by pedestrians on the 23 year old Essex Way. The house, now occupied by a former County Council chairman, is a legacy of Tudor and Stuart times when Coggeshall was a busy cloth manufacturing town. It is possible that parts of the Houchins upper storeys were workshops for worsteds, manikin or some other cloths.

REFRESHMENTS
The Chequers, The Street, Great Tey.

Walk 79   BRADWELL AND COGGESHALL   5½m (9km)

Maps: OS Sheets Landranger 168, Pathfinder 1076.

Astride the Blackwater Valley.

Start: At 825227, the Stockstreet lay-by on the A120.

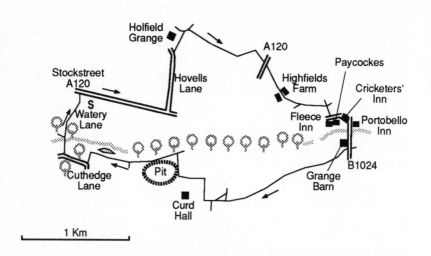

The lay-by can only be entered by westbound traffic. Eastbound vehicles need to use Coggeshall to turn around.

Go eastwards along the southern footway of the A120, then cross, with great care, to turn left, by a stand of pine trees, into Hovells Lane. Follow this to a white gate and stile, on the right, by more pines. Go over into the grounds of Holfield Grange and follow the slight causeway to the ha ha near the dovecote. Go over a stile and turn right along the track beyond to reach another stile. Go over and head south-eastwards, by a slight hollow, to a stile in a bend of the far hedge. Go over and follow paths through fields: at first go south-east to a new footbridge. Head ENE for the clump of foliage around a pond before the A120 fencing. Pass the pond's southern edge and go over a stile on to the A120. Cross, with great care, to a stile opposite. Go over and walk to Highfield Farm. Now from the trees by the beginning of the drive, head ESE

150

to the junction of two paths by trees around a pond. Go between allotment plots to reach a cross-paths by a brick wall.

Turn right along a track to the Fleece Inn and **Paycockes** in West Street, Coggeshall. Go left along the street, crossing Robinsbrook Bridge, then turning right by the Cricketers' Inn and right again by the Portobello Inn to a bridge over the Blackwater. Walk up Grange Hill to Grange Barn, and turn right on to Curd Hall Lane. At the end of the lane, turn right by the paddock rails, passing their northern side before dropping to the valley bottom with a gravel pit to the left. Cross a concrete road, with care, and go through a gap in the fencing. Turn left beside the riverside fringe of trees, going past the gravel pit, to the left, and a lagoon, to the right, then turning left, uphill, along a grassy headland. This joins Cuthedge Lane at an elbow bend: turn right to a wooded dell. Now turn right along Watery Lane, crossing a footbridge beside the ford. Cross a feeder where young trees provide handrails, and continue along the lane to return to the lay-by.

POINTS OF INTEREST:

Paycockes – This celebrated National Trust property in Coggeshall is a residence, but is open to the public during popular tourism times. It belonged to John, and then Thomas, Paycocke, master clothiers who moved to Coggeshall from Clare in about 1450. They operated an outwork system much loathed in many places, but respected as fair when run by the Paycockes. Great wool merchants had a habit of using their wealth to endow East Anglia with magnificent churches and superior dwellings. Paycocke Junior was no exception: he provided Coggeshall with one of each.

Also in West Street is the Isinglass factory of G P Swinborne & Co. The product is used for the clarification of beers and wines, but many local people remember using it to preserve eggs.

REFRESHMENTS:
The Fleece Inn, Coggeshall.
The Cricketers Inn, Coggeshall.
The Portobello Inn, Coggeshall.

Walk 80   HIGH EASTER AND GOOD EASTER   5¹/₂m (9km)

Maps: OS Sheets Landranger 167; Pathfinder 1098.

A Good Easter, High Easter shuttle across the district divide.

Start: At 638133, verge parking on Bedfords Road, Good Easter.

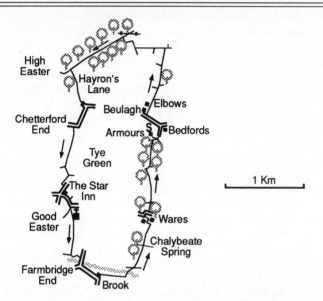

Walk westwards by Ravens to the red mail box at Beulagh. Turn right along a stony track by Elbows, passing the storage and other buildings. Beyond, the track is less stony, and over the district boundary it becomes a good High Easter headland, with a ditch on the right. At the ditch corner, the headland is unbridged: go left, beside the ditch, to reach the left-hand hedge, still on the same headland which is followed around the next bend to its end by a higher hedge under cables. Turn acutely left for six paces, then cross the field, right, to a footbridge enabling the footpath to cross a bridleway. Turn left along the bridleway, going through a gate into a large pasture. Follow the right-hand hedge to gate on to a bend of Hayron's Lane. Go left, uphill, to a junction marked by a dinosaur sculpture. Go right along the road, rounding a right-hand bend to reach a footbridge on the left. You are now back in Good Easter: follow a headland through two fields, and at the second junction of paths, turn right by garden hedges to reach Mill Road at Endway Cottage. Go right to reach the Star Inn at the village cross-roads. Turn left, passing a telephone kiosk, left, then Falconer Hall barns, and enter **St Andrew's churchyard**, on the right. There are two southside exits: go over the south-eastern footbridge to a path descending the Can valley to the north-west corner of a smaller field inserted in the larger one. Now follow the western side of a hedge to reach a footbridge. Go left and around a corner to reach a road. Turn right to cross Farmbridge over the Can and bear left towards Chalk End.

At the next (right-hand) bend, climb the banking on the left, by the chevrons alongside 2 Brook Cottages, and follow a path, with a hedge on the left, to cross the Can. Go left on the track to leave Roxwell and merge with another track near Chalybeate Brook. Ten paces downstream is a footbridge with white-capped posts. Cross this, and the field beyond to a fencing gap in the north-east corner. On the higher field edge, turn left to follow the Chalybeate watercourse upstream to Wares Farm. Follow arrows to turn right on the main drive. When in front of the farmhouse, use the drive to the left, by the paddock, under an arch of lime shrubbery, to reach Wares Road. Turn right around a double bend, then go left along a bridleway. Go over at a cross-paths, the double hedging giving way to double banking before more double hedging resumes after a staggered cross of footpaths in a dip. Approach Armours, going right to merge with a hard surface near a large store. Continue towards the silo, ignoring paths to the right to bend left and join the lane to Bedfords. Turn left to the start.

POINTS OF INTEREST

St Andrews Churchyard – St Andrew's elegant wooden spire is a pleasing landmark in the Can valley. Mainly dating from the 13th century, it belonged to St Martin's-le-Grand. Henry VIII gave it to Westminster Abbey. Inside there are memorials to the great and the good. Outside the confines of the churchyard, on a green, is a whipping post, a reminder of less fortunate times.

REFRESHMENTS
The Star Inn, Good Easter.

WILLINGALE $5^1/_2$m (9km)

Maps: OS Sheets Landranger 167; Pathfinder 1121 and 1122.
To the double churchyard of St Andrew and St Christopher.
Start: At 592090, verge parking near Shellow Bridge, Berners
Roding.

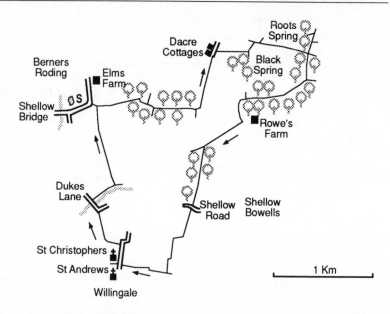

Follow the byway which leads eastwards away from the road. This becomes a
bridleway: follow it to its T-junction with another byway. Turn left to reach Dacre
Cottages, to the left. Just beyond, take a signed path on the right for Black Spring.
Cross a field aiming for the northern edge of trees. At their north-east corner, turn left
along a headland to a T-junction of headlands. Go right towards the long cluster of
trees around Roots Spring. At a junction with a tree-lined bridleway, go right, then
right again at a T-junction of bridleways. Follow the bridleway to Rowe's Farm lane.
Go right, then, just before a junction of metalled lanes, turn left along a bridleway,
following it to its junction with Shellow Road by a cottage dated AD 1870. Cross and
follow a path waymarked as part of the **Essex Way**. Go over a slatted bridge, walk

154

around the right-hand, concave corner and then swap sides of the western hedgeline by a hedge junction.

Walking towards cottages in front of Spains Wood, cross a bridge in the next corner and turn right. Another bridge swaps the path to the northern side of a high hedge. Enter the cricket field, following the same hedge to reach a fenced path into **Willingale**. Opposite is the churchyard twosome of St Andrew's and St Christopher's. Turn right to reach the former village school. Beside it, a path goes left by the garden and around a field to the lane for Dukes Farm, to the right. Turn left, cross a bridge, and opposite the ford's 'Unsuitable for Vehicles' notice, turn right at a footpath sign, mounting the bank and walking along the edge of a field above the stream. After about 400 yards, look for the re-instated path across the rising fields to the left. Aim for a cart-sized gap in the hedgerow and go across a smaller field to a double plank footbridge. Cross this and the field beyond to reach the byway walked on the outward route. Turn left to regain the start.

POINTS OF INTEREST:

Essex Way – The Essex Way is a long distance route from Epping Station on London's Central Line to Dedham and Harwich. It was created in 1971 by the Council for the Protection of Rural Essex. The initial route, produced by King Edwards Grammar School, Chelmsford, was quickly followed by others, notably one devised by Vernon Clarke of Colne Engaine, to use more field paths. The Regional Tourist Board's interest in the project died because of complaints about crop-blocked paths. By 1984 the Essex Area Ramblers' Association members were aroused by the project, which they further amended and extended to Harwich. The Rights of Way Act 1990 clarified path-blocking law, and in 1993 Ways Through Essex, a branch of the County's Planning Department, took the project in hand and provided a professional service in the form of path furniture and a printed guide.

Willingale – Willingale Spain, probably named after a Norman lord 'd'Espaignes' is represented by St Andrew's, the southern, older and smaller of the two churches. Successfully rescued by the Friends of Friendless Churches it is still used for special Palm Sunday services. Willingale Doe, probably named after a Norman lord 'd'Eau', is represented by St Christopher's, the larger and younger (by 200 years) church.

REFRESHMENTS

The Malsters' Arms, Willingale.

Maps: OS Sheets Landranger 167; Pathfinder 1121.
'... and men may go, but I go on for ever ...'
Start: At 579067, a lay-by near Little Whitney Green.

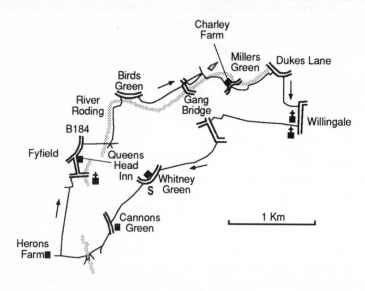

From the lay-by, follow a bridleway south-westwards to the valley of the Roding at
Cannons Green. Turn left along a road, then fork right at the end of the tarmac by
house No. 30 to follow a bridleway further down the valley. Fork right to the river
bank, then left to a bridge and right over a triple sleeper bridge. Follow the bridleway
out of the valley towards Herons Farm. About 200 yards from the farm, turn right by
a large oak tree on the right and follow a path northwards. Cross a triple plank bridge
and use a broad headland to approach a recreation ground. Downhill, right, a few
paces is an earthen bridge across the boundary ditch to the playing area: follow this,
then a hedge to reach Queen Street, Fyfield. Turn left, passing the school, left, and the
Queen's Head Inn to use the B184 sidewalk as far as the NRA depot by a bridge.
Cross the bridge and turn right over a stile. Follow the fence, left, to a concrete arch
over the River Roding. Cross and walk to a cross-paths. Turn left on a path that joins

the riverbank: follow the bank to Birds Green girder bridge. Cross to a road. Turn right for 200 yards, then right again along a signed path. The path is not clear, but runs parallel to the river to reach a road. Cross the road above Gang Bridge to enter the golf area. Cross to the riverbank and walk to a reservoir where signs indicate a footbridge used to swap to the southern bank.

Continue upstream to a footbridge over the right-hand ditch. Cross, turn left and follow the field edge to Charley Farm by Millers Green ford. Do not cross the footbridge beside the ford: instead, use the path beginning in the field with a concrete cartbridge. Pass to the south of Millers Green Farm and step left over a shallow ditch at the garden end to reach a tall hedge by a deeper brook. Follow the hedge upstream to the chicken run and kennels of the next garden. Follow the garden fence right around an old pit to a gap on to Dukes Lane. Turn right, uphill, to reach a signed path on the right. Follow the right edge to a copper beech, then grope along by the fencing of a former school, to emerge in Willingale. Turn right to the churchyard with a pair of churches separated by a footpath (*see* Note to Walk 81). Take the path, passing the war memorial and a splendid commemorative plantation donated by the local Women's Institute. The path continues to a valley. Bend left at the bottom to reach a bridge, cross and climb to a garden boundary. Follow it left to a bridge by a road junction. Turn left along the road to Chelmsford, going around the chevroned bend, then right over a footbridge. Cross a field to a cartbridge in a hedge gap. Cross the field beyond to Whitney Green and Willingale Road. Go left back to the lay-by.

POINTS OF INTEREST:
In 1899, early days for popular cycling, the rector Dr L E Lewis of Fyfield conducted short services for cyclists. It is reported that 800 attended, although it is not clear whether they all arrived for the same service.

REFRESHMENTS:
The Queens Head, Fyfield.
The Black Bull, Fyfield.
The Malsters Arms, Willingale.

Walk 83   PAGLESHAM   5¹/₂m (9km)

Maps: OS Sheets Landranger 178; Pathfinder 1143.
By a reedy and creekside wilderness.
Start: At 944923, the Plough and Sail Inn, Paglesham East End.

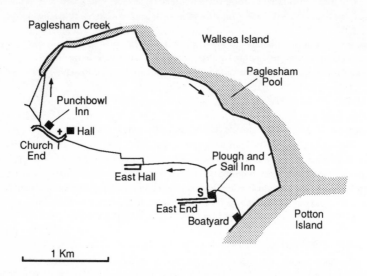

Follow the unmade road beside the Plough and Sail Inn, continuing ahead from its first, right-hand, bend on a path which heads northwards, threading through Well House garden to meet a track. Take this westwards, then turn right, as waymarked, at East Hall to pass the eastern and northern sides of the barns and so reach a headland behind. Turn left at the first junction to pass the face of one of many 'Private' signs in the locality. An excellent field-edge path now leads to paddock rails and a drive to Church End.

Bear left, passing the Punchbowl Inn, and then turn right along a concrete drive which serves a sub-station. From the pumphouse, continue along the grassy headland by some young trees to reach the seawall of **Paglesham Creek**. This is not exactly the right of way from Church End to the seawall, but it is a good, nearby and well-used substitute when the mid-field route is not available. Should the real path be re-instated it clearly has precedence over the headland by the young trees.

Go right along the elevated walk to Paglesham Pool. Given good visibility, the height of the seawall allows extensive views over the Crouch and Roach rivers to the churches at Canewdon, Althorne and Foulness. Warehouses dominate Wallasea Island and south-facing facades of Royal Yacht Clubs line Burnham's seafront. Both Potton and Foulness Islands are occupied by MoD structures. Five stiles punctuate the wall path which bends to contain the mud of the Roach in a broad channel. Winter is a fine time to be here, though the east winds are liable to bring tears to the walker's eyes. Skirt the oyster beds and enter J W Shuttleworth's Boatyard. Steps lead down to the concrete slipway: pass carefully through the landside yacht storage area and follow the unmade road back to the Plough and Sail.

POINTS OF INTEREST:
Paglesham Creek – The unusual plants around the estuary are those which can resist the saltiness of the inter-tidal environment. Some thrive on the saltmarshes yet are not able to prevent erosion of the marshes into mudflats. Look for sea lavender, sea purslane, cordgrass and samphire. Essex saltmarshes and mudflats support waders almost all the year round. Look for oystercatchers, bar-tailed godwits, curlews, dunlin, knot, shelduck and redshanks. Brent geese depart after Christmas.

Human activity could include the well-tried art of smuggling. Whilst customs and excise regulations exist, so will smugglers, attempting to beat the system. Brandyhole Creek is just around the corner as a reminder of former exploits.

Unobtrusive, positive waymarking is complete and helpful at all the strategic places around this route. The concrete 'public footpath' posts and their newer black plastic replacements are placed by the local authority and take precedence over any other displayed signwriting. Although the posts are sometimes vandalised, local ramblers, operating an 'Adopt a path' policy, keep watch over developments and maintain the path furniture up to date. Numbers on the posts refer to parish path numbers: each path has a number just as motorways do.

REFRESHMENTS:
The Plough and Sail Inn, Paglesham East End.
The Punchbowl Inn, Paglesham Church End.

Walk 84   LITTLE YELDHAM   5¹/₂m (9km)

Maps: OS Sheets Landranger 155; Pathfinder 1028 and 1051.

A circuit on the Colne – Stour watershed.

Start: At 789425, verge parking on Bakers Road, Belchamp
St Paul.

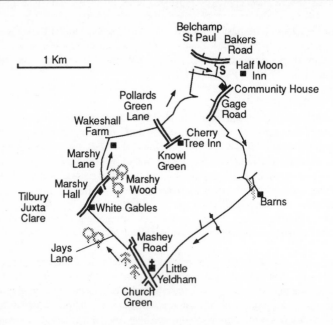

Head southwards along a path reached by steps cut in the bank. Pass a pond and
follow a hedge under wires to reach a footbridge. Cross and go left, mid-field, leaving
the field to cross some rough grasses between the **Community House** and the recreation
ground, **Belchamp St Paul**. Turn right along Gage Road as far as Path 25, opposite
Gage's House. Turn left along this headland to reach the farther side of a small wood.
Now swap sides of the hedge and look for the ditch ending in the left-hand field.
Aligned with the ditch is a bridge, over which a swap back to the eastern side of the
hedge may be made. Go through a gap at the next hedge junction. Follow the field
edge, using the nearby cartbridge of a concrete road where the correct bridge is missing.

Follow a brook towards some grey barns, but before they are reached, turn right along a path that crosses a blue girder footbridge from the left. After a few steps, cross a culvert bridge to the southern side of the ditch. Now follow the ditch uphill, passing under the pylons near the crest and going through several fields to reach St John the Baptist's Church at Little Yeldham.

Turn right along Church Green and climb Mashey Road ahead. A stand of conifer trees marks the junction of unmade **Jays Lane** by a double bend of Mashey Road: go left, then bend right with the lane, going away from the trees and continuing uphill past a spinney, wide hedges and leafy ponds, to reach Belchamp Road by bend-warning chevrons in Tilbury-juxta-Clare. Turn right, passing White Gables and Mashay Hall, right, to reach the beginning of Marshy Wood. Turn left along Marshy Lane, passing some restored black barns to reach a T-junction with a drive. Turn right, passing picturesque Wakeshall Farm, right, to reach Pollards Green Lane. Cross this, going slightly left to reach Path 28. Cross a narrow field to a double plank bridge with handrails and steps to an upper field. Gage's House is in view again: leave it to the right as you cross mid-field heading north-eastwards to a hedge junction. Go over a bridge and follow the right-hand hedge until it bends away. Now cross mid-field, under the pylons, to reach another hedge bend. Pass to the left of a pond to reach a bend of grassy Workers Lane. Go left, northwards, along this bridleway towards Lovelands Farm. When you are about 400 yards short of the buildings clustered along Bakers Road, turn right at a cross-paths to follow a re-instated crosspath eastwards for 400 yards to reach a sleeper bridge in a hedge bend. Cross and walk with the hedge on your left to reach a similar bridge in the next corner, the one used earlier on this walk. Now re-trace the outward route back to the start.

POINTS OF INTEREST:
Community House – This is a recent addition to village facilities. It is shared by five other local parishes, and it is managed by the trustees of a gift from the owners of Moyns Park in Birdbrook.
Belchamp St Paul – The church is dedicated to St Andrew, even though the village is named after St Paul's, London, sometime owners of much land in the village.
Jays Lane – Lane widths in Little Yeldham in 1770 were reckoned to be 30 feet wide between ditches 2 feet deep. Jays Lane has shrunk a little since then, especially at the Tilbury end.

REFRESHMENTS:
The Half Moon, Cole Green, Belchamp St Paul.
The Cherry Tree, Knowl Green, Belchamp St Paul.

Walk 85   LEIGH-ON-SEA $5^{1}/_{2}$m (9km)

Maps: OS Sheets Landranger 178; Pathfinder 1161 and 1162.
Thameside Cockle sheds and Belton Hills Country Park.
Start: At 811875, John Burrows Car Park, Rectory Road, Hadleigh.

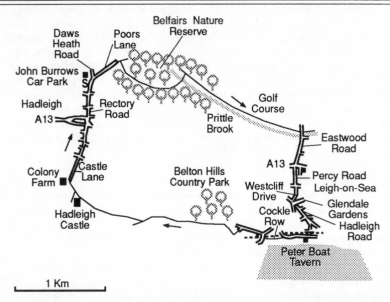

Walk along Poors Lane, which completes the junction with Rectory Road and Daws Heath Road. It is a cul-de-sac dipping to Belfairs Lane. The Lane has poles carrying wires aloft, and a subsidiary path forks right to a gate of Belfairs Nature Reserve. Take this, entering the Reserve and following the path by the backgarden fence of Shepherd's Walk for a few paces before forking left on a lovely leafy path under tall trees. Pass the Hodges' seat and turn right to cross a bridge at a T-junction. Climb the gravel path to a crossing and go left to descend to the valley of Prittle Brook, a tributary of the River Roach. The Reserve is a retreat for humans too, and there are commemorative seats available for contemplation beside the permissive paths. Maintain the descent at the next T-junction, cross a bridge and leave the Reserve to join Belfairs Trotting Track, downstream beyond the trees. Continue to the fringe of a golf course. Follow Prittle Brook to Eastwood Road at an NRA sluice station. Turn right to traffic lights at the junction with the A13. Cross, with care, to Percy Road which descends towards the Thames Estuary. Continue on Westcliff Drive and Glendale Gardens before climbing Hadleigh Road to cross Marine Parade. Now bear right and descend steeply to the New Road footbridge over the railway track.

On the southside is the Peter Boat Tavern, and south of that a promenade which curves westward under the flyover to reach **Cockle Row** by a shell beach. Climb the steps to Leigh-on-Sea railway station, cross the bridge and go along Belton Way West. Enter cut-off Castle Drive, and from its western end take the mid-field path to reach Belton Hills Country Park. Follow the Park's southern boundary, then re-enter the same field, using the headland to approach the whaleback hill graced by **Hadleigh Castle**. Climb to the top stile. The castle is not actually in Hadleigh Country Park, but between the Belton Hills and the Kersey Vale sections of it.

Go over the stile on to a lane and turn right, dipping north to Colony Farm. There, go over another stile on to Castle Lane. Follow this road to High Street's pedestrian crossings by St James' Church. Now follow Rectory Road back to the car park.

POINTS OF INTEREST:

Cockle Row – The Row attracts artists like the seashells attract gulls. Cocklers still unload their boats after 400 years of activity by walking a plank pliant, with each footfall straining under the yoke of a double basket, to deliver the catch to the cooking sheds. The Port of London health authority oversees the preparation of shellfish dredged from beyond Leigh Creek.

Hadleigh Castle – The castle dates from 1230 when Henry III granted his chief political officer, Hubert de Burgh, permission to build. It was rebuilt in 1360 by Edward III with a high curtain wall and eight towers, plus an elaborate barbican. Catherine of Aragon owned it, as did Anne of Cleeves and Katherine Parr. The castle became a ruin in the 17th century, and was been damaged by landslips. Later, a Constable painting of the scene won acclaim.

REFRESHMENTS:

The Peter Boat Tavern, Leigh-on-Sea.
There are numerous other possibilities in Leigh-on-Sea and Hadleigh.

Walk 86   STANFORD-LE-HOPE   5¹/₂m (9km)

Maps: OS Sheets Landranger 177; Pathfinder 1161.
Overlooking a big bend of the Thames.
Start: At 683825, Victoria Road Car Park, Stanford-le-Hope.

Leave 20 Victoria Road along Path 36 heading east to cross King Street. Go past another car park and climb to St Margaret's Church, joining Church Hill at the Rising Sun Inn. Go left, then right across The Green to the Clinic. Now follow Wharf Road, passing the cemetery to dip under a railway line. A pylon guards a double footpath sign: double back, right, towards the railway at its level and bear left across Stanford Warren pitscape. Cross a footbridge over Mucking Creek and continue to a road by Mucking Church. Go along Mucking Wharf Road, over the level-crossing and turn right along Butts Lane as far as the first pylon. Between two further pylons a green path climbs left. Look back from the summit at the broad Thames over Yanlet channel, between Canvey and Grain Isles. The path peters out atop the rabbit warren: stay arable side of an earthen wall around the spread of another pit-cum-tip. Follow the linear heap northwards, then westwards to reach a stile on to Buckingham Hill Road.

Turn right to the A1013. Cross, with care, and go left along a stiled track between the A13 and A1013 roads to a bridge.

Turn right over the bridge and follow the farm track beyond to Saffron Garden Farm. Go ahead, with wires showing the way, left of a ditch, to **Hordon-on-the-Hill's** recreation ground. Go east along Orsett Road to the church. Squeeze between the yard walls east side of the church to join High Road by the village hall, pump and Swan Inn. Turn right, passing the Bell Inn and descending South Hill to the speed limit sign. Path 37 begins left off Pump Street as a drive to two dwellings, then passes a paddock. Cross a field divide to reach arable land. Well used, the perimeter path neglects the direct line to the exit under wires by a Horndon House track. Head for the roadway embankment, with a hedge on the left, to reach a stile. Go over, mount steps and turn left to the top of the ramp. To the right, above the dual carriageway, are central refuges which aid a perilous crossing over the A13 and the A1013. Go right along the latter's verge as far as lamp post 94 where the crash barrier is stiled. Descend a handrailed staircase and walk beside the brook. Cross a footbridge by the railway bank and continue downstream to pass under the railway. Go over the brook, then over a confluence bridge. Now follow the high industrial fences to 19 Victoria Road, **Stanford-le-Hope,** the Constitutional Club and the start.

POINTS OF INTEREST:
Horndon-on-the-Hill – The village has several 400 and 500 year old houses by its 700 year old church. Thomas Highbed was a village hero in 1555 when he suffered death by burning for his faith.
Stanford-le-Hope – Frequent references are made to Hassenbrooks, a Jacobean manor, to the castellations of St Clere's Hall, and to beautiful St Margaret of Antioch Church, but it is nearby Mucking where secrets of pre-history may yet be undisturbed. The first big bend of the Thames waterway was an easy landing place and archaeologists worked hard to establish facts about former settlements on sites now extracted and infilled with refuse or converted to pitscapes as at Stanford Warren.

REFRESHMENTS:
There are several possibilities in Hordon-on-the-Hill and Stanford-le-Hope, including those mentioned in the text.

Walks 87 & 88 JACQUES BAY AND BRADFIELD ARCH 6m (9½km) or 8m (13km)

Maps: OS Sheets Landranger 169; Pathfinder 1053 and 1078.
Foreshore footprints on the flotsam line.
Start: At 176314 Station Road, Wrabness.

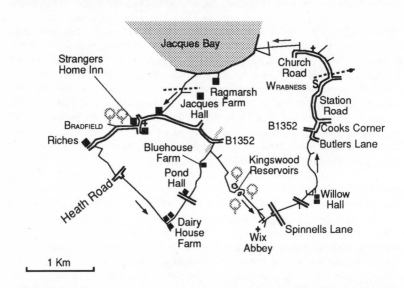

Walk along Station Road, then turn left into Church Road. Down the slope beyond the church is a sharp left bend: here a track goes right, beside Shrublands, towards the Ness. Go over a stile and turn left behind a garden hedge. Now cross a grassy headland towards **Jacques Bay**, crossing the service road to the beach huts, to meet the sea at the end of Wall Lane. Walk along the curve of Jacques Bay, by bridleway, adjacent to the footpath, or the foreshore if the tide allows. After passing a hide, erosion has played havoc with parts of the path to Ragmarsh Farm. Just beyond the farm, a track leads inland towards Jacques Hall. Leave the foreshore here, but turn right off the track to follow a path across a field, heading towards the arch in the railway embankment. Go through the arch on to a path heading south-westwards to a back garden stile in Bradfield. Follow the path beyond to a road.

The shorter walk turns left here. Follow the road to a bridge over a brook. Just beyond, turn right along a footpath that goes upstream to a hedge junction. The longer walk rejoins here.

The longer walk turns right along the road to reach a T-junction at St Leonard's Church, Bradfield, opposite the Strangers Home Inn. Turn left, then right by the Community Centre to follow Mill Road. Opposite 'Riches' turn left over a plank bridge. Follow a garden fence and then the change crop line to reach the fence corner. About 100 yards right there is a stile on the original line of the path: go over and cross fields to reach Heath Road by Street Farm. Turn left, then soon, right, into Dairy House Lane. Go over a brook, past a reservoir and climb to Dairy House. Turn left to pass face-side of the B&B signs and follow the drive out to reach Bradfield Road by Pond Hall. Turn right, then left along a garden boundary towards Bluehouse Farm. Pass to its left, continuing to reach the hedge junction where the shorter route is rejoined.

Go up the southern side of the left hedgerow, pass a footbridge and find the exit bridge just round the concave corner. Now follow the right-hand hedge to the twin Kingswood reservoirs. Cross the causeway between them and wheel around to the eastern side to follow a headland towards Wix Abbey. Swap sides of the hedge at the track crossing, then go over a footbridge on to a sub-station track. Go left to Spinnells Lane. Cross and follow a path towards a white post marking a bridge. Cross and follow the path beyond to Willowhall Lane. Cross this and the field beyond to reach a stile. Follow a field edge towards Willow Hall, using a gate to reach a track leaving the farm. Now walk NNE with a ditch on your left. Cross the next field to pick up the curving left-hand boundary. Go over a bridge and follow the left-hand hedge to reach Butlers Lane at a bend. Turn left to reach the B1352. Turn right to Cooks Corner. There, turn left into Station Road, following it back to the start.

POINTS OF INTEREST:
Jacques Bay – The Royal Navy's former Mine Depot by the railway alongside the Bay was purchased in 1993 by The Wrabness Nature Reserve Charitable Trust.

REFRESHMENTS:
The Strangers Home Inn, Bradfield.
The Village Maid , Bradfield.
The Wheatsheaf, Wrabness.
The Black Boy, Wrabness.

Walk 89   CRESSING   6m (9½km)

Maps: OS Sheets Landranger 167 and 168, Pathfinder 1075 and 1076.

Messing about on field paths near Cressing.

Start: At 810225, verge parking in Church Road, Bradwell.

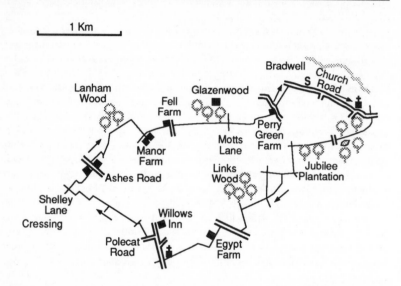

Walk south-eastwards along the road, passing the church and going into a dip. Go right into the waymarked gravel pit entrance, going under the power cables. Where the vehicles bend left to a weighbridge, bear right between a hedged brook, on the right, and a grassed tip, on the left, to reach Sheepcotes Lane. Cross the road and follow a path beside a ditch, passing Jubilee Plantation to reach a bridged cross-paths. Turn left, uphill, and cross a hedge at the top to walk westwards along the field edge towards Clapdog Green. At the end of the hedge on the right, turn left on an alternative field edge path which goes around to the southern end of a ploughed-out path. Stay with the hedge to reach a path junction south of Links Wood. Go left, following the hedge to Boars Tye Road. Turn right, then left along Egypt Farm drive. The waymarked route around the farm differs from that on the Pathfinder map, but guides you clearly to a road at Cressing Church. Turn right to the triangular green (**the Willows Inn** is straight ahead), and left there, along Polecat Road. Soon, take a waymarked path to the right. The path chicanes left-right to reach a bridge to the next field. Follow a hedge to a stile, go over and cross to another stile. Follow the path beyond, bearing left to reach a sleeper bridge into the next field. Follow a ditch to another sleeper bridge in the field's northern corner. Cross to Shelley Lane: go right for a couple of paces beside the ditch just crossed, and then follow the eastern side of the lane's hedge to a pylon. Turn right, now with the ditch on your right. Cross the next field boundary to reach Ashes Road beside Bloomsberry. Turn left to Sideways, turning right there on a path through an old orchard. Turn right in a hollow and follow the left hedge around to a headland which becomes a track beside Lanham Wood. Follow the track to Lanham Lane. Turn right as far as a fuel tank on piers. There turn left into a field, head towards Manor Farm Cottage's hedge, then go left on a path aligned with overhead wires.

Cross Lanham Green Road by Fell Farm and maintain direction across three fields, passing **Glazenwood** in the third. Muddy Motts Lane is avoided by following a headland towards Perry Green Farm. The headland swaps sides of a hedge before swinging uphill to go beyond the poultry houses. Turn right for the exit by the farmhouse opposite the pond. Turn left along a road to reach a waymarked path on the right. Go NNE across a field, crossing on the change-crop line parallel with the left hedge to reach a stile. Go over and descend past a drinking trough to a stile on to Church Road. Turn right to the start.

POINTS OF INTEREST:

The Willows Inn – This 400 year old inn stocks good East Anglian ale and serves food six days a week. One evening per week live country and western music can be heard there.

Glazenwood – This stylish house shares the same name as the woodland surrounding it. Established as a market garden specialising in herbs of renown after World War I, today the house and garden are opened to visiting parties.

REFRESHMENTS:
The Willows Inn, The Street, Cressing.

THE LEIGHS 6m (9¹/₂km)

Maps: OS Sheets Landranger 167, Pathfinder 1098.
In the sylvan valleys of river and brooks.
Start: At 719168, Rest Harrow Corner, Little Leighs.

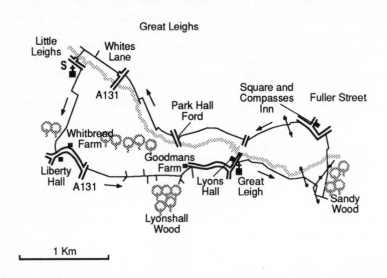

Walk past the church and turn right to the white gates set back off the road by a lagoon. Go through and follow the right-hand hedge, swap via a mid-field strip to follow the left-hand hedge in the next field. Go over a stile and follow a worn path south-westwards to a bridge over Straw Brook by a spinney. Climb a lane which levels out on to concrete by Whitbread Cottages. Turn left along Whitbread Farm Lane, passing Liberty Hall to reach the A131. Cross, with care, and follow a path along the hedge on your left to reach a footbridge. Cross and follow a mid-field path, converging with the right-hand ditch. Cartbridges at a complex of ditches and headlands allow you to continue eastwards towards a stand of young conifers. Cross a gravel track, maintaining direction along an intermittent hedgerow to reach a headland north of Lyonshall Wood. Cross a shallow ditch and chamfer off the corner of the next field, passing to the right of the trees around Goodman's Farm to reach a road. Go right to the thatched pump cover, then left along Boreham Road to Lyons Hall and the Great Leighs war memorial. Now take a path on the right, on the far side of **Great Leigh's church**, which drops diagonally down to continue downstream along the riverbank for several fields, leaving the **valley** when you are under the minor of two sets of pyloned cables. Climb up the slope to the right, going under the major set of cables and following an eastward headland.

At the beginning of Sandy Wood, turn left to re-enter the valley. Go under the major set of cables again and cross a footbridge over the Ter. Pass a copse, to the right, and follow a ditch to the road in Fuller Street. Turn left: passing a turn to the Square and Compasses, on the right. Turn left by the garage of Brook Cottage on to a mid-field path up to an embankment. Go left along the bank and swing right under the minor set of power cables to use a beautiful grassy headland to reach the 1881 spring by Boreham Road. Cross and follow the path opposite, going through the pastures of the Ter valley. Go past stables and down steps to a road at Pork Hall ford. Turn right, uphill, for a few paces then go left on a path across more grassland and along the left hedges of arable fields. At the sewerage treatment compound, go down to the river beside the fencing. Ignore both the footbridge and the vehicular bridges, staying on the path along the field edge to reach the A131. Cross, with care, into Whites Lane. Turn left to pass Keeper's Cottage and cross the Ter to reach Rest Harrow Corner again.

POINTS OF INTEREST:
Great Leighs Church – The church has a rounded tower of the sort more common in Norfolk than Essex, there being only five others in the East Saxon territory. The three-stage tower houses five bells founded by Miles Gray in 1634. There is much fine craftsmanship to be seen in and around the church, not least the Norman arches.
Valley – Osiers are basketry willows grown in good draining, well-watered rooting areas, such as the Ter valley. One variety, Salix purpurea, shows an attractive reddish colour in late winter sunshine. Rooted stumps sprout clusters of saplings up to 5 feet high. These are harvested annually and can either be barked or boiled to produce pliant lengths of cane, either white or buff in colour.

REFRESHMENTS:
The Square & Compasses Inn, Fuller Street, Fairstead.
The Dog & Gun, Great Leighs.

Maps: OS Sheets Landranger 167; Pathfinder 1121.
Stanford Rivers and Cripsey Brook Country.
Start: At 553032, Budworth Hall car park, Chipping Ongar.

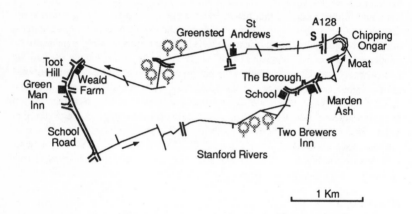

Follow Bansons Lane, which leaves High Street opposite the Cock Inn. Go past the
library and cross Cripsey Brook. Climb the path to **St Andrew's Church**, Greensted.
Cross the Greensted Hall drive and go around the next field to a stile into a small
field. Cross to a gate. Go through, walk past lime trees, and turn right through Greensted
Hall Farm, going downhill on a track to a footbridge level with the last building. Turn
left and follow the right hedge through three fields to a double bridged exit on to a
road. Cross and follow the path opposite climbing across a field to reach a stile that
takes the path left of a small spinney. Continue over six further stiles through paddocks
to reach a T-junction by the farm with amusing warnings. Go right and follow the
right hedge towards Toot Hill. As Weald Farm is approached the path is bridged to
the northern side of a cottage garden, then bends around the last out-building to cross
by Weald Lodge and join Toot Hill Road at a bend. Turn left, passing the Green Man

Inn, then forking left, by the telephone kiosk, along School Road. Descend to reach the Stanford river by a junction. To the left is a signed path: follow this to a path junction by a hedge corner. Home-made waymarks now take you down to a cartbridge by a willow tree. Cross this and the field beyond to join Coleman's Farm drive. Go right, between the farm and a bungalow, then turn left through a slide-bar stile on to a bridleway.

Follow waymarks towards Newhouse. Go right of a hedge to join another path and cross paddocks using three stiles. After crossing Mutton Row, continue over further stiles and bridges then go along the hedge on the left, swapping sides as far as a belt of trees near Kettlebury Spring. Go over a parish boundary bridge in the trees, then cross a field, going under wires to reach the south-east corner of a school field. Descend a lane along the school fence turn right along The Borough to the Two Brewers Inn. Turn left, cross Cripsey Brook and the A128, with care, into Bushy Lea. Take the left of two paths from the stile at the eastern end, and go left again up by the Castle Vineyard. Turn right by Rosedale and enter Spring Meadow by the lamp. Follow the path around the **outer moat**, then, when north of Castle House, use a permissive path, signed 'Ongar Castle', left, to reach Budworth Hall.

POINTS OF INTEREST:
St Andrew's Church – This famous church has nave walls with split oak trunks as studs, now partially infilled to display the structure. It has survived, with restoration, since at least 1013 when the body of the martyred King Edmund, first patron saint of England, was rested here en route from London to Bury St Edmunds.
Outer moat – The remaining mound of Chipping Ongar Castle is about 40 feet high: the water-filled moat arcs around part of its 60 yard diameter base. The castle was a regional base for King Henry II.

REFRESHMENTS:
The Cock Tavern, Chipping Ongar, on the route.
The Green Man Inn, Toot Hill, on the route.
The Two Brewers Inn, on the route.

Walk 92   **EPPING**   6m (9$\frac{1}{2}$km)

Maps: OS Sheets Landranger 167; Pathfinder 1121.

Bell Common, Coopersale Street, Steward's Green and Ivy Chimneys.

Start: At 450010, Bell Common car park, Forest Side.

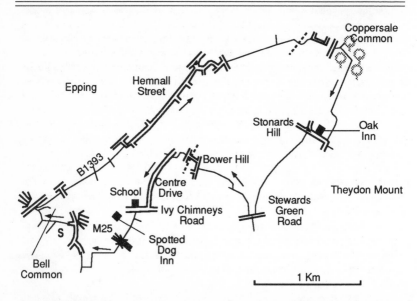

Go through the bridleway gate beside the small car park and follow the the hoggin-dressed track past the fringe of trees, swinging left to the heart of the forest. Leave it at a bend continuing ahead by a couple of white post markers and turning right by more markers around a cricket field. Railings mark the vehicular entry to the pavilion: use the track, bearing left by a large pond. Walk north-eastwards across **Bell Common**, crossing a disused path and Theydon Road to join Hemnall Street, Epping at a bend, by The Lodge. Hemnall Street runs parallel to the High Street and there are several connecting alleys and snickets: follow it across Station Hill and dip to merge with Palmers Hill by the Epping Forest Council Offices. Go right, up Theydon Grove, just before these Offices and swing left above a pond. Go right and left on the residential sidewalks, then cross Stonards Hill to reach steps to the recreation ground. Continue

174

north-eastwards across the games area, going south of the hospital. Go over a bridge at a path junction and cross a field to a bridge over the railway. Follow the path to No. 2A Vicarage Road. Turn right to reach a snicket going right from No. 24 to reach Coopersale Common by St Alban's church hall. Take the bridleway beside South View and fork right at a path junction just inside a kissing gate. The path threads through shrubbery and goes over a couple of slatted walkways to reach a waymarked stile and footbridge by a field boundary on the right. Cross and follow a path across two fields. Turn left to a stile, go over and continue to reach a road at a bend, by The Lodge. Turn right, passing the Theydon Oak Inn to reach a triangular road junction. Turn left on to a bridleway, following it to a road at Steward's Green.

Turn right, go past Nos. 57 and 56 and then turn right along a path that follows a ditch, right, to a cartbridge. Cross a field towards the flat roofs of Bower Court. Go past rear garden fences to reach Bower Hill. Turn right, uphill, then turn left to Hillcrest Way and a footbridge over Epping Railway Station. Now follow a snicket that begins between the car park and the coalyard and rises to Centre Drive. Turn left along the road to a T-junction with Ivy Chimneys Road. Turn right to a school. The Spotted Dog Inn is ahead, but the route takes the path opposite the school, beside No. 68. Cross a bridge at the rear of the gardens and climb along the fence, right, to go under power cables and over the M25. Beyond this, go over a stile on the right and cross to a stiled gate before Great Gregories Farm. A statutory diversion is waymarked. Go south across a concrete drive and along a fenced headland for 90 yards to a stile. Go over and turn right across a field to a stile on to another headland. The path becomes surfaced: turn right along Great Gregories Lane/Theydon Road, but just before the motorway tunnel parapet, turn left into Forest Side to regain the car park.

POINTS OF INTEREST:

Bell Common – The cricket field here was removed whilst the motorway was constructed in a cutting. When completed, the cutting was covered to create a tunnel and the cricket field was re-instated.

REFRESHMENTS:
The Forest Gate, Bell Common.
The Theydon Oak Inn, Coopersale Street.
The Spotted Dog, Ivy Chimneys.

Walk 93   **DOVERCOURT**   6$\frac{1}{2}$m (10km)

Maps: OS Sheets Landranger 169; Pathfinder 1054 and 1078.
A walk by two coastlines, one industrial, one recreational.
Start: At 237310, Dovercourt Church.

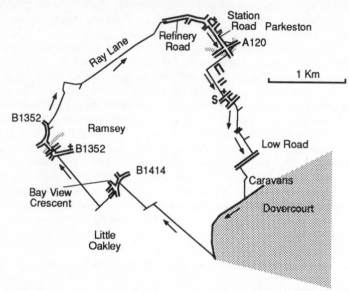

Cross Main Road to enter Laurel Avenue. Cross Long Meadow to reach a paved path passing behind a community hall to join Halfacre Lane. Continue SSE through a thorny habitat, across an estate road and beside school fencing to Holmleigh on Low Road. Turn right as far as Keynes Way. Turn left along a fenced lane around a **holiday camp** and caravan park. From the south-west corner of the fence, follow a path across a field to a borrow dyke bridge. Slowly mount the seawall to get a peep of the waders before they see you. Now follow the elevated path towards Bramble Island, bending left with the wall over South Hall Creek culvert. At the next left bend, alongside Long Bank drain, drop from the wall and turn acutely right to face Oakley ridge. A path begins beside the drain and then crosses a field to a small covert. Continue north-westwards to go over a footbridge at the intersecting field boundary. Now walk to a T-junction of paths by a hawthorn bush. Go left, as waymarked, and right at the next

176

boundary junction. Follow the hedge on the right-hand side to reach the B1414 by Burnthouse Farm. Cross the road carefully and turn left by the opening to Lodge Road and Bay View Crescent.

Keep the two roads on the right and Harwich Road on the left, going along a track by a clubhouse car park. The track becomes a path beyond the sports ground: after about 200 yards, turn right along a path which links with a hedgerow to drop off the ridge down a change-crop mark. Pass Whinney Grove and join Church Hill via a parking lot. Go straight over at a roundabout into Ramsey's Main Road. Fork right by the Castle Inn to follow Wrabness Road to reach the second of two close footpath signs pointing right. Follow the left-hand field edge, then cross the re-instated line of the next field, and go between boundaries when down by East Newhall. Steer around garden fences and between barns, as waymarked, to join Ray Lane. Follow the lane eastwards to reach Refinery Road. Bear right to join West Dock Road, continuing to reach Station Road by a church. Turn right, away from the liner-ferries looming large over **Parkeston Quay**, to reach a roundabout on the A120. Turn east towards Harwich as far as the end of the footway railings, then cross the road, with care, and descend the bank to the west side of Ramsey Creek. Walk beside the brook, going under the brick bridge of Parkeston Road to reach a footbridge which carries the path to the southern side of the creek. Continue south-westwards, shielded from A120 by overlap fencing. Cross Norway Crescent's open space and, at the end of the housing, turn left, uphill, by the back garden fences. The path levels out and returns you to the start.

POINTS OF INTEREST:

Holiday camp – The successful television sitcom series *Hi Di Hi* was filmed at this site.

Parkeston Quay – This is the terminal for Harwich and the Continent trains from Liverpool Street. Ferries that a decade ago used Felixstowe, Harwich and Parkeston are now largely concentrated at the specialist ferry port at Parkeston, leaving Harwich with a heavy roll on, roll off schedule, and allowing Felixstowe to develop as the largest container port in the United Kingdom.

REFRESHMENTS:

The Castle Inn, Ramsey.
The Captain Fryatt, Garland Road, Parkeston.
The Bird in Hand, Dovercourt.
The White Horse, Dovercourt.

Walk 94   **TAWNEY COMMON**   6¹/₂m (10km)
Maps: OS Sheets Landranger 167; Pathfinder 1121.
Where trees once spread from the Lee to the Roding valleys.
Start: At 499012, verge parking on Tawney Common.

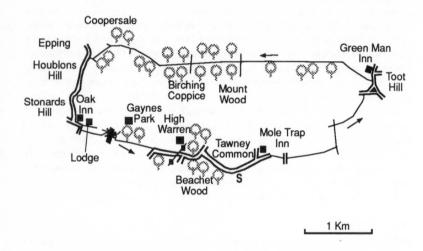

Walk eastwards along the verge, passing the Mole Trap Inn, and continuing east to
just beyond a black barn where a gateway on the right leads to a field. Follow a path
to a stile by a broken sign. Go over, cross the road beyond, and use a cultivation mark
to reach a footbridge. Cross the next field to a cartbridge by a hedge junction. Follow
the right hedge of the next field to the Scots pine by a derelict barn. A grassy track
now converges with the stream to the left at a bridge by a junction with a bridleway.
Turn left, up the hedged track, going about 70 yards beyond the overhead cables to
reach a gate on the right. Go through and cross a field to a stile into a paddock. Cross
to another stile. Go over and follow waymarks up and over a golf course to a stile on
Epping Road. Go right to Toot Hill's triangular junction, bearing left to reach a signed
path on the left by the telephone, postbox and hydrant. The Green Man Inn is just
ahead.

178

Leave the garden fence corner in the meadow and cross to a stile in the north-west corner. Go over and follow the right hedge to a cross-paths. Go ahead to reach a stile down the slope by a spinney. Vestigal trees of the cleared forest now line the headland up to the cross-tracks of Colliers Hatch. Go ahead, through Ongar Park Wood, over the banks that signal Theydon Mount's boundaries, and into the rhododendrons of **Birching Coppice**. Go over the M11 and descend to Gernon Bushes, a woodland nature reserve. Follow the main path WNW for 200 yards to a signpost pointing left. Take this line between holly shrubbery on to Coopersale Common recreational area. Stay woodland side by the school fence and go through the kissing gate by St Alban's church hall. Turn left down Houblons Hill to a T-junction. Turn left to pass Theydon Oak Inn. At a sharp right bend, go ahead on a bridleway parallel with Gaynes Park drive. Go over the M11 and continue beside parkland. Two fields later reach a road at a bend. Go ahead, taking the second turn right, around Beachet Wood to Tawney Common and the start.

POINTS OF INTEREST:
Birching Coppice – The coppice management of woodland involves the cutting of trees just above ground level. Then, after about twenty years, the new growth is cut to produce a harvest of poles. Young tender growth shooting through from ground level is easily grazed off by deer. The solution is to coppice at a higher level above nibbling mouths. This is pollarding. The woodlands of West Essex have many examples of fine beech pollards.

REFRESHMENTS:
The Mole Trap Inn, near the start.
The Green Man Inn, Toot Hill.
The Theydon Oak Inn, Theydon Mount.

Walk 95   WALTHAM ABBEY   6½m (10 km)

Maps: OS Sheets Landranger 166 and 167; Pathfinder 1120 and 1121.

A walk by the Lee Valley Countryside project.

Start: At 383008, Harold Bridge Car Park, Waltham Abbey.

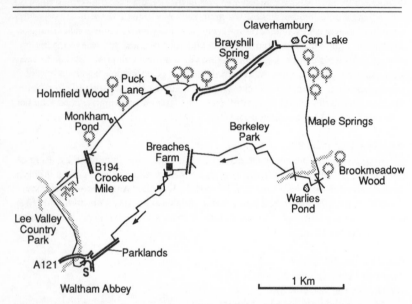

Cross the Greenwich Meridian sign to the building with an information shop and toilets, passing to its left. Cross a bridge and go under the A121. Bear right to Cornmill Stream, following it to its confluence with Old River Lee. Turn right over a footbridge and follow strong Government fencing to the end of the cypress hedge. Join the newly created Meridian Walk, heading northwards to a statue, then going right to reach the B194 (Crooked Mile) and to leave the **Lee Valley Country Park**. Do not follow the bridleway on the opposite side of the road: instead, take the footpath to the left of it, leaving the blackened road behind Eagle Lodge to climb through a thicket, recross the tree-lined road. Now cross a field, uphill, to a waymark by an oak in a vestigal row of trees. Go over a stile by Monkhams pond and go downhill across a field at the edge of Homefield Wood. Go through a gap between wood and hedge, then cross a field to reach a bridged junction with Puck Lane about 200 yards before a pylon. Follow the lane to Galleyhill Green and then another blackened road to reach another road. Turn left, passing Brayshill Spring, left, to reach the pet cemetery of Claverhambury. Bear right along an unmade road as far as the carp lakes, then turn right, by a transformer, along a path, using wriggle-through or step-over railings as stiles to link a series of pastures. The path rises beside Stocking Grove and descends by Scatterbushes Wood to a stile and slatted bridge by Maple Springs.

Cross three more pastures (the first two along the left hedge, the third along the right) then bear right to a footbridge over Cobbins Brook in Brookmeadow Wood. The woodland path is clear, and on leaving the trees there is a fine view of Upshire church. Follow the hedge, right, to a bridge, cross and bear left to a pond. Turn right, still hedgeside, then bear left to bridge re-crossing Cobbins Brook. Continue westwards to a stile by a gate. Go over and turn right to go through a waymarked gate to a water tank on stilts. Pass a glasshouse and turn left on the track by the transformer and chimney. Pass more glasshouses and continue to a road. Turn left to reach a T-junction with Galleyhill Road. Go left. Ignore a signed path, left, but take the one on the right. Go around a convex corner by a barn and head westwards aiming for a line-carrying pole at a hedgerow corner. Follow the right hedge down, west, then south, to a bridge in the bottom corner. Follow the ditch to the right to a cartbridge under the power lines. Turn left and go around the next corner to a plank bridge. Now follow the right-hand hedge across a fen-like field to the garden fencing behind Hereward Close. Cross an improvised bridge on to a road (Parklands). Turn right to the roundabout beside the car park.

POINTS OF INTEREST:
Lee Valley Country Park – The Park was set up in 1967. It stretches 23 miles along the Lee from the Thames to the Stort, and within it some 10,000 acres of land and water have been regenerated for sport, leisure and conservation.

REFRESHMENTS:
There are numerous places in Waltham Abbey.

Walk 96   LANGHAM   7m (11km)

Maps: OS Sheets Landranger 168, Pathfinder 1053.
By Black Brook and a Hidden Valley.
Start: At 025332, verge parking in Dedham Road, Langham.

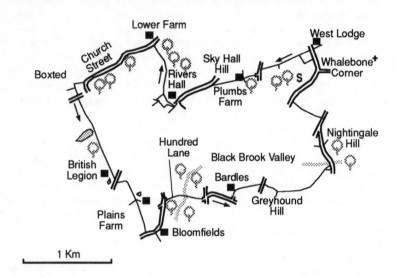

Walk back towards Gun Hill as far as Whalebone Corner and go left, downhill, into
the **Stour Valley** on the lane to Low Lift. By West Lodge, a path crosses the road.
Turn left, heading WSW along this to reach a bridge. Cross and follow the edge of the
field beyond. Cross the next field to reach Alderton Lane at a waymark. Almost opposite
is the drive to Plumbs Farm: take this, passing to the south of the steading and crossing
a field from the hedge corner to reach the upper gateway on Sky Hall Hill. Turn left,
uphill, then turn right for Rivers Hall and enter a field to the left to pass to the south
side of most of the buildings, rejoining the drive by a pond. Go down the drive and
cross the dam of a lake to reach Lower Farm Road. Turn left, uphill, continuing along
Church Street to St Peter's Church. Just before the church, turn right on a path, near
Aubrey Cottages, to reach the school. Turn left along School Lane, then cross Church

Road into the drive of Pond House. Fork left of the house, cross a dam and climb to a stile. Follow the path beyond to reach Straight Road.

Cross to the path opposite and follow it past Plains Farm, to the left. Continue along the path to Chapel Road. Turn left along the road, then right on to the Hundred Lane byway. Dip and rise through wooded Black Brook valley and, at a T-junction, turn left, but soon go right along High Street. Walk as far as Serenity, then turn left along a drive by the tennis court and follow the waymarkers to the right of Bardle Barn. Cross two fields to a road at Greyhound Hill. Cross to the drive opposite, following waymarks through gates and over stiles around a smallholding, through a spinney, above the fishery, and down to a road at the foot of Nightingale Hill. Turn left, re-cross Black Brook and follow the road, ignoring waymarks to the left and right of Rectory Road. At a staggered crossing of footpaths, turn left and head towards the waymarked gap in the Dedham Road hedge. Turn right along the road to return to the start.

POINTS OF INTEREST:

St Mary's Church, Langham – John Constable's friend was curate at Langham, and through him he knew the rector, John Fisher, who became Bishop of Salisbury. Constable's paintings include both Salisbury Cathedral and St Mary's Church. The hut in the churchyard was established in 1832 as a little church school for girls of the parish poor.

Stour Valley – When footpath and bridleway traffic were the main forms of land transport, waterways were important arteries for heavy haulage. The Stour was important because it passed through prosperous agricultural and woollen trading places. In 1628 Charles I granted Letters Patent for the creation of a navigable river, and this was followed in 1705 with an Act of Parliament to the same effect. In 1968 the River Stour Trust was formed to protect and enhance public navigation of the river from Manningtree to Sudbury.

REFRESHMENTS:
The Shepherd & Dog, Langham.
The Wig & Fidgett, Boxted.

Maps: OS Sheets Landranger 167; Pathfinder 1121.
In the shadow of Copped Hall glories.
Start: At 431999, Lodge Road car park, off the B1393.

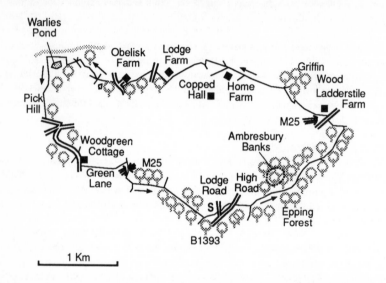

Between the car park and High Road (the B1393) is a hoggin-dressed bridleway: follow it north-eastwards, crossing the B1393 and continuing towards Ivy Chimneys, passing **Ambresbury Banks** to the left. Turn sharp left to Forest Side when the cricket pavilion is in view. Cross a gutter-bridge on the outside of the bend and follow white-post waymarkers for another bridleway in the fringe of the tree canopy. Go left for a couple of posts, then emerge right to cricket boundary. Cross High Road to a path between Ladderstile Farm and the M25 tunnel parapet. Go over a ladder stile and cross a field to a stepless stile. Walk along the left edge of Griffin Wood to reach an estate road. Go left as far as the cross-tracks between Home Farm and White House, then turn right for a couple of paces and go over a stile on the left to follow a waymarked path to Lodge Farm. To the right here is **Copped Hall**. Go over a footbridge and follow the hedge to the left to an estate track. Follow the track to a grassy forest tract to the left of Lodge Farm. Now follow a worn path to a road. Cross and follow a hedge on your right past Nicholls Farm going half a field away from the obelisk, to reach a lane at Obelisk Farm.

Turn right then left at the next waymarker. Go past a wood-fringed anglers' pond and a landscaped garden to reach a track. Cross and follow the eastern and northern edges of the next large field to reach Cobbins Brook bridge beyond Warlies Ponds. Anglers' paths encircle the ponds, offering several options to join the southern exit path. Do not cross the bridge: instead, follow the wooded boundary out of the valley and swap to the grazing side of a hedge over a green stile. Walk south to reach Pick Hill by a double-poled support for overhead wires. Turn left, downhill, crossing Upshire Road into Woodgreen Road. Follow this as far as Woodgreen Cottage. There, turn left along Green Lane, crossing the M25. Now, where the unmade road swings south as Woodredon Farm Lane, continue eastwards. Drop to a brook and climb to enter the St Thomas Quarter of Epping Forest. Follow intermittent white posts to a junction with another hoggin bridleway, within the sound of High Road traffic. Turn left and cross a bridge and re-join Lodge Road by the car park.

POINTS OF INTEREST:

Ambresbury Banks – This is an Iron Age hillfort excavated in 1882 by members of the, then 2 year old, Essex Field Club, led by General Pitt-Rivers. Here, according to local lore, Boadicea, following ultimate defeat by the Romans, fled to take her own life.

Copped Hall – In 1987 the Friends of Copped Hall Committee was formed to preserve the vestigal buildings and some land around it, such is the appeal of its history. Early occupants of the Hall served as Royal Huntsmen of the Forest. It is known that Mary Tudor stayed at Copped Hall for some time, that William Shakespeare presented *A Midsummer Night's Dream* in the Long Gallery and that Princess Anne sheltered in the Hall during the troubles of 1688 when William of Orange landed at Brixham.

REFRESHMENTS:

None on the route, but available in nearby Epping and Waltham Abbey. Also close by is the *Sixteen-String Jack Inn*, in Theydon Bois Forest, an inn reputedly named after a highwayman.

Walk 98   BURES TO SUDBURY   7m (11km)
Maps: OS Sheets Landranger 155; Pathfinders 1029 and 1052.
A linear walk in beautiful Stourdale.
Start; At 902340, the station in Bures Hamlet.

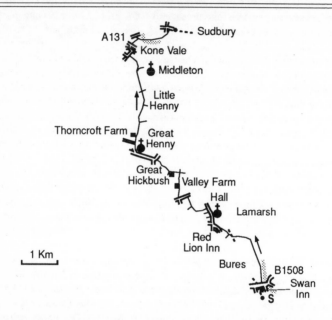

Sudbury is the terminus of a branch line from Colchester via Marks Tey: Bures is the
next stop towards Colchester. Trains between the two are approximately hourly and
there is also a bus service along the B1508.

Bures Station is little more than a platform situated high above Station Hill:
descend the hill to find the Swan Inn at the corner of Bridge Street. Turn left opposite
the inn along a path by a red brick wall to join a track beyond the wall. Follow the
track to reach a stile just before a meandering loop of the River Stour is reached. Go
over and turn left to a stiled level crossing of the railway track. Go up the lane beyond
to Bell Hill in Lamarsh. Turn right, passing the Red Lion. Turn right to pass the old
pump, the old school and the church to reach Lamarsh Hall and Hall Farm. Turn left
along a headland by the transformer on stilts. Follow it uphill, pausing occasionally to

186

admire the view over Stourdale. At the top, swing right along the ridge heading northwards to reach a charming tree-lined country lane. Go left to a T-junction. There, go through the gate on the right and down to Valley Farm. Go through a gate, over a stile and descend a gully path to join a track by a horse trough. Follow the track downhill for a few strides, then go over a stile on the right and continue to descend, now close to the eastern side of the farmhouse.

Go over a double-bridged stile in the valley, cross the field beyond and climb the bank to go left as far as Great Hickbush. Turn right along the drive to a road and walk ahead towards the church on a hump above Stourdale, passing the Rectory to reach a kissing gate north of the churchyard. Go through and descend, with Thorncroft Farm on your left. Go over several stiles as you head northwards through paddocks. Go over bridges to the west of Applecroft Farms and continue northwards through Little Henny to reach the high crosspaths of Middleton (at 869393). Go over, following a headland downhill, with Middleton church on the right. From the headland's bottom bend, climb to a stile on the next ridge. Go over and head for the rooftops of Pinecroft Rise to reach a stile. Go around the top edge of an old chalk quarry to the back garden fences. Continue to the play area and follow Meadow View Road around to Middleton Road. Go over the stile opposite and cross Kone Vale to the embankment of an old railway line. Climb this and turn right along The Valley Walk, crossing the river Stour and passing The Quay Theatre to reach the swimming pool adjacent to **Sudbury** station.

POINTS OF INTEREST:

Bures – Bures consists of three parishes. The main one, Bures St Mary is in Suffolk, the other two are in Essex but in separate districts. The people of Bures can therefore have fun comparing the performances of their three representative Members.

Sudbury – This is a jewel of a town with much to see and do. Thomas Gainsborough lived and painted here.

REFRESHMENTS:

The Swan Inn, Bures.
The Red Lion, Lamarsh.
There are also several possibilities in Sudbury.

Walk 99   THE WOODHAMS   8m (13km)

Maps: OS Sheets Landranger 168; Pathfinder 1123.

A walk in the Lower Chelmer Valley.

Start: At 839056, a lay-by on the A414 south of Maldon.

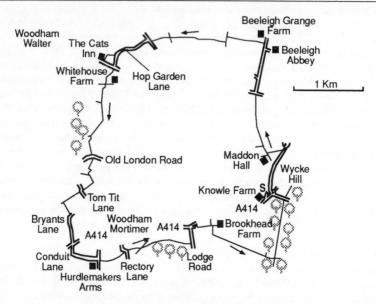

Use the footway beside the A414 to head up Wycke Hill towards Maldon, going as far as the drive, left, to Maldon Hall just before the next roundabout. Take the drive, approaching the cluster of buildings over two cattle grids. Swing right to leave the drive between Headlands and the barn dwellings. A gravelled drive leads through a new plantation and under power cables to follow a hedge, on the left, to reach London Road by a reservoir earthbank. Cross the road and follow the lane opposite, dropping to the Chelmer valley. Just after passing **Beeleigh Abbey**, to the right, turn left along the field path on the southern side of Beeleigh Grange Farm. Follow the right-hand, low hedge into the next field, maintaining direction to go under the power cables and on to a footbridge. Cross and turn left up a lane to the next field junction, on the right. There, turn right and continue westwards, beyond a ditch source to the left, to reach a bridge. Cross and continue, now with a ditch on right. Swap sides of the ditch at a cartbridge, walk past a spinney and continue towards Woodlands. Where the track swings right of the dwelling, a path forks left to pass to the left of the garden fencing. Cross the drive by a white picket fence and maintain direction along a field edge. Cross a mid-field section, then go along Guys Farmhouse hedge to reach Manor Road. Turn right, but soon turn left along Hop Garden Lane, following it to a T-junction with Curling Tye Lane. The Cats Inn is to the right here. Cross and go along Whitehouse Farm drive, passing to the right of the main buildings. Head southwards over a crossing track and follow a ditch to the source.

Continue south-westwards along a mid-field path (Path 16) to the trees of The Wilderness. Resume a southwards direction parallel with the woodland edge, passing through a gap in a crossing hedge and following the field edge around to a stile by cottages. Go over and follow their drive to Old London Road. Go along Lodge Farm drive opposite, following waymarks through the buildings to cross a stiled bridge 100 yards south of the farmhouse. Turn right to follow a brook through two fields and the chicane of Tom Tit Lane to reach a drive to the north of Brook Cottages. Approach Thrift Wood, turning left 100 yards before the trees. Go over several stiles and walk beside a garden to reach Bryants Lane. Turn right to reach a cross-roads with the A414. Cross, with care, and go along Conduit Lane to a T-junction. The Hurdlemakers Arms are to the right here. Cross and follow the footpath opposite to Rectory Lane. Go right, then left on a path that follows the double hedges to a double-stiled crossing path. Go left and follow the right-hand hedge through three fields, chamfering the right-hand corner of a fourth to reach Hazeleigh's Lodge Road. Turn left to reach the A414 just by the cut-off of an old elbow bend. Turn right along the old road and continue ahead, off the bend, for a few paces to reach a footpath sign on the right. Follow the path southwards for 100 yards to reach a pole, where it turns left and crosses the field, going under wires, to reach a ditch bend. Follow a ditch to the embankment of an old railway line. The footpaths have been transferred from the bottom of the bank to the top thanks to the enlightened local nature reserve management. Turn left and enjoy the elevated walk as far as the steps down to a road crossing. To the left is Knowle roundabout at the foot of Wycke Hill.

POINTS OF INTEREST:
Beeleigh Abbey – The remains of a 12th-century Premonstratensian abbey have been incorporated into a private residence.

REFRESHMENTS:
The Hurdlemakers Arms, Woodham Mortimer.
The Cats Inn, Woodham Walter.

Walk 100   BILLERICAY TO BRENTWOOD   9m (14½km)

Maps: OS Sheets Landranger 177; Pathfinder 1141 and 1142.

A linear walk by the Crouch headwaters.

Start: At 675950, Billericay Station.

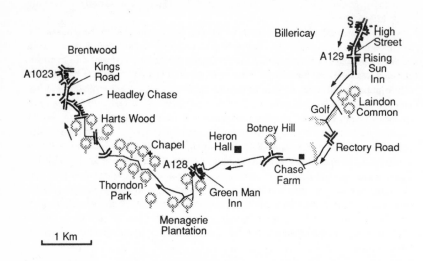

The return train journey from Brentwood to Billericay, completing this fine walk, takes only six or seven minutes. It is also possible to return by bus.

From the station, go right along Radford Way and right again to cross the track and climb High Street to the A129 junction by the Rising Sun Inn. Cross and walk down Laindon Road to reach a path on the right by the school. Follow the right-hand hedge to a lane. Go left into Frithwood. A right turn is clearly indicated over the golf course: follow the right-hand boundary until a footbridge allows a swap to the northern bank of the young River Crouch. Continue to a pond, and there go SSE across another section of the golf course to reach a stile. Go over and follow a path to Laindon Common Road. Turn right, cross Clock House Road and follow Rectory Road, soon reaching a left bend. Two paths emanate from the bend: one follows the road on the fieldside of the hedge, the other follows the garden hedge, and then heads south-westwards across a field. Follow the latter path, passing from hedge corner to hedge corner and the right-hand hedge to reach an incised valley twisting left and down to a footbridge. Cross and go right, downhill, then left, brookside, to a cartbridge. Cross and follow a mid-field track, heading WSW to the earthbanks and equipment bays south of Chase Farm. Turn right towards the farm and go over a stile on the left. Cross the foot of a paddock to a matching stile. Cross the field towards Botney Hill.

Go over a stile and follow the southern fence to reach Green Lane some 30 yards away from a corner. Turn right, then left along Billericay Road towards Herongate. Pass Blind Lane, then turn right along a path just before Parkhill Wood. Follow the path northwards to a ditch, cross and turn left along it. Go over several footbridges and cross the drive to Heron Hall. Continue along the ditch for three fields to reach the black barn of Fouchers Farm. Turn right along a track and go left by the first hedge. The path squeezes between hedge and rails, rounding the waterworks dwelling to meet a drive. Follow this to Cricketers Lane and turn right opposite the Green Man Inn, crossing the A128, with care, to enter Park Lane. West of the opening greensward is a stile: go over and walk through woodland to Menagerie Plantation. Follow the Plantation's northern edge, cross a stream and turn right on a path between golf and Woodland Trust activities to reach a junction of tracks south of the chapel at 615913. Continue past the Countryside Centre to reach a road at the Lion Gates. Cross and maintain direction through Harts Wood to reach Hartswood Road. Turn right, cross a bridge and turn left on a path heading westwards through Donkey Lane Plantation. After 400 yards, turn right to the Guardsman Close exit. Turn left along Woodman Road, then right along Headley Chase. Turn right again along Kings Road to reach **Brentwood** station.

POINTS OF INTEREST:
Brentwood – Early this century a molecatcher named Oddy would call at a Brentwood inn for his weekly drink. When finished he would search in his deep pocket for a rabbit, display and sell it, and with the proceeds refill his glass. Sometimes this process recurred until he knew no disappointment.

REFRESHMENTS:
The Green Man, Herongate, on the route.
There are also numerous possibilities in both Billericay and Brentwood.

TITLES IN THE SERIES